My Travel Journal

This journal belongs to

_____

TABLE OF CONTENTS
—

INTRODUCTION

—

My Travel Journal was born out of memory. As I sat down to write a new book, I went in search of the journal from my first round the world trip. There, buried down deep in my drawer, was a little book filled with memories long forgotten. Names, places, dates, expenses. Things I thought happened one day occurred, in fact, months later. People and important relationships were totally forgotten by the sands of time. Cool experiences had been cobwebbed over.

Flipping through those old pages, I remembered the drunk nights at that hostel bar in Prague with my new best friends, the smell of setting foot in a Thai food market for the first time, the unforgettable closeness I felt squeezed into that bus in Cambodia, watching the sun rise on a new year in Belize, and the pure joy and wonder that I felt every day I was on that trip.

That journal represented memory.

But, as I read it, I couldn't help but think how much more I could have added.

Life as a writer has taught me that journaling is more than simply writing things down. People tend to gloss over the ugly parts, aren't introspective enough, forget the small things, and, generally, just don't know *how* to journal.

My Travel Journal features pre-, during, and post-trip prompts to help you organize your thoughts, feelings, and remember what you saw, who you met, and what you did. It helps guide you to develop the skill of journaling.

That way, years from now, when you stumble across this book and sit down to relive your own life changing memories, you'll remember all those crazy moments that were lost to the sands of time and be happy you took my advice to write everything down.

Sincerely,

Matthew Kepnes

NomadicMatt.com

HOW TO USE THIS JOURNAL
—

Journaling might seem straightforward but it is a skill. It's more than writing down what you did and then calling it a day. Great journaling requires introspection, honesty, and consistency.

And travel offers anything but consistency.

Here are our tips on how to get the most out of this journal:

1. Be consistent – Try to write before bed every day so your thoughts are fresh in your mind. If that's not possible (because you went out), try to write before you go out or during breakfast. Set a time to make sure you always do it.

2. Be detailed – The more detailed you can be about what you saw and what you did, the better this journal will become. Don't take shortcuts or be lazy. Write down everything. You will forget it otherwise. Trust us.

3. Be honest – No one is going to see this journal but you. There's no reason to hide your true self. Be honest about how you feel, what you did, and where you failed. The more honest you are with yourself, the more you will grow as a person.

PRE-TRIP THOUGHTS
—

Use this section to organize your thoughts, goals, desires, and hopes for your future self. This section will help put into focus what you really want to get out of your trip.

Twenty years from now you will be more disappointed by the things you didn't do than by the ones you did do.

So throw off the bowlines, sail away from the safe harbour. Catch the trade winds in your sails.

Explore. Dream. Discover.

— H. Jackson Brown

On this trip, I'll be gone from _____ to _____.

On this trip, I will be going to:

_____

_____

_____

On this trip, I want to learn:

01. _____

02. _____

03. _____

04. _____

05. _____

On this trip, I want to do:

01. _____

02. _____

03. _____

04. _____

05. _____

I am most excited to visit: _____

I am most scared about:

_____

_____

The biggest fear I want to conquer is:

_____

_____

On this trip, I want to accomplish these 3 personal development goals:

01. _____

02. _____

03. _____

My total budget for this trip is: _____

I affirm these committments to myself:

Yes, I will push myself to do new things.
Yes, I will push myself to make new things.
Yes, I will go with the flow.
Yes, I will be ready to change plans.
Yes, I will try new foods.
Yes, I will learn to be comfortable being uncomfortable.
Yes, I will push myself out of my comfort zone.
Yes, I will learn not to worry about what others are thinking.
Yes, I will remember that other people can do this, so can I.

Date: _____
Signature: _____

TRIP THOUGHTS
—

"Would you please tell me, which way I ought to go from here?"

"That depends a good deal on where you want to get to," said the cat.

"I don't much care where ... " said Alice.

"Then it doesn't matter which way you go," said the cat.

— Lewis Carroll

DATE: _____   **PLACE:** _____   **BUDGET:** _____

---- ✦ ----

3 things I did today:

01. _____

02. _____

03. _____

Favorite thing I ate today:

_____

One person I met today (name, age, where they are from):

_____

One thing I learned about the world today:

_____

One thing I learned about myself today:

_____

One thing I will do different tomorrow:

_____

General thoughts about today:

_____

_____

_____

DATE: _____   **PLACE:** _____   **BUDGET:** _____

"Travel is about the gorgeous feeling of teetering in the unknown."
— Anthony Bourdain

3 things I did today:

01. _____

02. _____

03. _____

Favorite thing I ate today:

_____

One person I met today (name, age, where they are from):

_____

One thing I learned about the world today:

_____

One thing I learned about myself today:

_____

One thing I will do different tomorrow:

_____

General thoughts about today:

_____

_____

_____

DATE: _____ **PLACE:** _____ **BUDGET:** _____

---✦---

3 things I did today:

01. _____

02. _____

03. _____

Favorite thing I ate today:

_____

One person I met today (name, age, where they are from):

_____

One thing I learned about the world today:

_____

One thing I learned about myself today:

_____

One thing I will do different tomorrow:

_____

General thoughts about today:

_____

_____

_____

DATE: _____ **PLACE:** _____ **BUDGET:** _____

"Life is either a daring adventure or nothing at all."
— Helen Keller

3 things I did today:

01. _____

02. _____

03. _____

Favorite thing I ate today:

_____

One person I met today (name, age, where they are from):

_____

One thing I learned about the world today:

_____

One thing I learned about myself today:

_____

One thing I will do different tomorrow:

_____

General thoughts about today:

_____

_____

_____

DATE: _____   **PLACE:** _____   **BUDGET:** _____

———————————— ✦ ————————————

3 things I did today:

01. _____

02. _____

03. _____

Favorite thing I ate today:

_____

One person I met today (name, age, where they are from):

_____

One thing I learned about the world today:

_____

One thing I learned about myself today:

_____

One thing I will do different tomorrow:

_____

General thoughts about today:

_____

_____

_____

DATE: _____   **PLACE:** _____   **BUDGET:** _____

"The life you have led doesn't need to be the only life you have."
— Anna Quindlen

3 things I did today:

01. _____

02. _____

03. _____

Favorite thing I ate today:

_____

One person I met today (name, age, where they are from):

_____

One thing I learned about the world today:

_____

One thing I learned about myself today:

_____

One thing I will do different tomorrow:

_____

General thoughts about today:

_____

_____

_____

DATE: _____ **PLACE:** _____ **BUDGET:** _____

---------------------------◆---------------------------

3 things I did today:

01. _____

02. _____

03. _____

Favorite thing I ate today:

_____

One person I met today (name, age, where they are from):

_____

One thing I learned about the world today:

_____

One thing I learned about myself today:

_____

One thing I will do different tomorrow:

_____

General thoughts about today:

_____

_____

_____

DATE: _____   **PLACE:** _____   **BUDGET:** _____

"All our dreams can come true, if we have the courage to pursue them."
— Walt Disney

3 things I did today:

01. _____

02. _____

03. _____

Favorite thing I ate today:

_____

One person I met today (name, age, where they are from):

_____

One thing I learned about the world today:

_____

One thing I learned about myself today:

_____

One thing I will do different tomorrow:

_____

General thoughts about today:

_____

_____

_____

DATE: _____   **PLACE:** _____   **BUDGET:** _____

---✦---

3 things I did today:

01. _____

02. _____

03. _____

Favorite thing I ate today:

_____

One person I met today (name, age, where they are from):

_____

One thing I learned about the world today:

_____

One thing I learned about myself today:

_____

One thing I will do different tomorrow:

_____

General thoughts about today:

_____

_____

_____

DATE: _____   **PLACE:** _____   **BUDGET:** _____

"Happiness is when what you think, what you say, and what you do are in harmony."
— Mahatma Gandhi

3 things I did today:

01. _____

02. _____

03. _____

Favorite thing I ate today:

_____

One person I met today (name, age, where they are from):

_____

One thing I learned about the world today:

_____

One thing I learned about myself today:

_____

One thing I will do different tomorrow:

_____

General thoughts about today:

_____

_____

_____

DATE: _____ **PLACE:** _____ **BUDGET:** _____

———————————— ✦ ————————————

3 things I did today:

01. _____

02. _____

03. _____

Favorite thing I ate today:

_____

One person I met today (name, age, where they are from):

_____

One thing I learned about the world today:

_____

One thing I learned about myself today:

_____

One thing I will do different tomorrow:

_____

General thoughts about today:

_____

_____

_____

DATE: _____ PLACE: _____ BUDGET: _____

"How is it possible to feel nostalgia for a world I never knew?"
— Ernesto Che Guevara

3 things I did today:

01. _____

02. _____

03. _____

Favorite thing I ate today:

_____

One person I met today (name, age, where they are from):

_____

One thing I learned about the world today:

_____

One thing I learned about myself today:

_____

One thing I will do different tomorrow:

_____

General thoughts about today:

_____

_____

_____

DATE: _____ **PLACE:** _____ **BUDGET:** _____

---◆---

3 things I did today:

01. _____

02. _____

03. _____

Favorite thing I ate today:

_____

One person I met today (name, age, where they are from):

_____

One thing I learned about the world today:

_____

One thing I learned about myself today:

_____

One thing I will do different tomorrow:

_____

General thoughts about today:

_____

_____

_____

DATE: _____ PLACE: _____ BUDGET: _____

"If there is no struggle, there is no progress."
— Frederick Douglass

3 things I did today:

01. _____

02. _____

03. _____

Favorite thing I ate today:

_____

One person I met today (name, age, where they are from):

_____

One thing I learned about the world today:

_____

One thing I learned about myself today:

_____

One thing I will do different tomorrow:

_____

General thoughts about today:

_____

_____

_____

DATE: _____   **PLACE:** _____   **BUDGET:** _____

———————————— ✦ ————————————

3 things I did today:

01. _____

02. _____

03. _____

Favorite thing I ate today:

_____

One person I met today (name, age, where they are from):

_____

One thing I learned about the world today:

_____

One thing I learned about myself today:

_____

One thing I will do different tomorrow:

_____

General thoughts about today:

_____

_____

_____

DATE: _____   **PLACE:** _____   **BUDGET:** _____

"You go away for a long time and return a different person – you never come all the way back." — Paul Theroux

3 things I did today:

01. _____

02. _____

03. _____

Favorite thing I ate today:

_____

One person I met today (name, age, where they are from):

_____

One thing I learned about the world today:

_____

One thing I learned about myself today:

_____

One thing I will do different tomorrow:

_____

General thoughts about today:

_____

_____

_____

———————————◆———————————

3 things I did today:

01. _____

02. _____

03. _____

Favorite thing I ate today:

_____

One person I met today (name, age, where they are from):

_____

One thing I learned about the world today:

_____

One thing I learned about myself today:

_____

One thing I will do different tomorrow:

_____

General thoughts about today:

_____

_____

_____

DATE: _____ **PLACE:** _____ **BUDGET:** _____

"The traveller sees what he sees. The tourist sees what he has come to see."
— G.K. Chesterson

3 things I did today:

01. _____

02. _____

03. _____

Favorite thing I ate today:

_____

One person I met today (name, age, where they are from):

_____

One thing I learned about the world today:

_____

One thing I learned about myself today:

_____

One thing I will do different tomorrow:

_____

General thoughts about today:

_____

_____

_____

DATE: _____ **PLACE:** _____ **BUDGET:** _____

———————————◆———————————

3 things I did today:

01. _____

02. _____

03. _____

Favorite thing I ate today:

_____

One person I met today (name, age, where they are from):

_____

One thing I learned about the world today:

_____

One thing I learned about myself today:

_____

One thing I will do different tomorrow:

_____

General thoughts about today:

_____

_____

_____

DATE: _____ **PLACE:** _____ **BUDGET:** _____

"Everything you can imagine is real."
— Pablo Picasso

3 things I did today:

01. _____

02. _____

03. _____

Favorite thing I ate today:

_____

One person I met today (name, age, where they are from):

_____

One thing I learned about the world today:

_____

One thing I learned about myself today:

_____

One thing I will do different tomorrow:

_____

General thoughts about today:

_____

_____

_____

DATE: _____   **PLACE:** _____   **BUDGET:** _____

—————————— ✦ ——————————

3 things I did today:

01. _____

02. _____

03. _____

Favorite thing I ate today:

_____

One person I met today (name, age, where they are from):

_____

One thing I learned about the world today:

_____

One thing I learned about myself today:

_____

One thing I will do different tomorrow:

_____

General thoughts about today:

_____

_____

_____

DATE: _____ **PLACE:** _____ **BUDGET:** _____

"Don't tell me how educated you are, tell me how much you have travelled."
— Mohammed

3 things I did today:

01. _____

02. _____

03. _____

Favorite thing I ate today:

_____

One person I met today (name, age, where they are from):

_____

One thing I learned about the world today:

_____

One thing I learned about myself today:

_____

One thing I will do different tomorrow:

_____

General thoughts about today:

_____

_____

_____

DATE: _____   **PLACE:** _____   **BUDGET:** _____

———————————◈———————————

3 things I did today:

01. _____

02. _____

03. _____

Favorite thing I ate today:

_____

One person I met today (name, age, where they are from):

_____

One thing I learned about the world today:

_____

One thing I learned about myself today:

_____

One thing I will do different tomorrow:

_____

General thoughts about today:

_____

_____

_____

DATE: _____ **PLACE:** _____ **BUDGET:** _____

"Life is beautiful if you are on the road to somewhere."
— Orhan Pamuk

3 things I did today:

01. _____

02. _____

03. _____

Favorite thing I ate today:

_____

One person I met today (name, age, where they are from):

_____

One thing I learned about the world today:

_____

One thing I learned about myself today:

_____

One thing I will do different tomorrow:

_____

General thoughts about today:

_____

_____

_____

DATE: _____ **PLACE:** _____ **BUDGET:** _____

---✦---

3 things I did today:

01. _____

02. _____

03. _____

Favorite thing I ate today:

_____

One person I met today (name, age, where they are from):

_____

One thing I learned about the world today:

_____

One thing I learned about myself today:

_____

One thing I will do different tomorrow:

_____

General thoughts about today:

_____

_____

_____

DATE: _____ **PLACE:** _____ **BUDGET:** _____

"Jobs fill your pocket. Adventures fill your soul."
— Jamie Lyn Beatty

3 things I did today:

01. _____

02. _____

03. _____

Favorite thing I ate today:

_____

One person I met today (name, age, where they are from):

_____

One thing I learned about the world today:

_____

One thing I learned about myself today:

_____

One thing I will do different tomorrow:

_____

General thoughts about today:

_____

_____

_____

DATE: _____   **PLACE:** _____   **BUDGET:** _____

———————————◆———————————

3 things I did today:

01. _____

02. _____

03. _____

Favorite thing I ate today:

_____

One person I met today (name, age, where they are from):

_____

One thing I learned about the world today:

_____

One thing I learned about myself today:

_____

One thing I will do different tomorrow:

_____

General thoughts about today:

_____

_____

_____

DATE: _____ **PLACE:** _____ **BUDGET:** _____

"Good company in a journey makes the way seem shorter."
— Izaak Walton

3 things I did today:

01. _____

02. _____

03. _____

Favorite thing I ate today:

_____

One person I met today (name, age, where they are from):

_____

One thing I learned about the world today:

_____

One thing I learned about myself today:

_____

One thing I will do different tomorrow:

_____

General thoughts about today:

_____

_____

_____

DATE: _____ **PLACE:** _____ **BUDGET:** _____

———————————◈———————————

3 things I did today:

01. _____

02. _____

03. _____

Favorite thing I ate today:

_____

One person I met today (name, age, where they are from):

_____

One thing I learned about the world today:

_____

One thing I learned about myself today:

_____

One thing I will do different tomorrow:

_____

General thoughts about today:

_____

_____

_____

DATE: _____ **PLACE:** _____ **BUDGET:** _____

"I met a lot of people in Europe. I even encountered myself."
— James Baldwin

3 things I did today:

01. _____

02. _____

03. _____

Favorite thing I ate today:

_____

One person I met today (name, age, where they are from):

_____

One thing I learned about the world today:

_____

One thing I learned about myself today:

_____

One thing I will do different tomorrow:

_____

General thoughts about today:

_____

_____

_____

DATE: _____ **PLACE:** _____ **BUDGET:** _____

———————◆———————

3 things I did today:

01. _____

02. _____

03. _____

Favorite thing I ate today:

_____

One person I met today (name, age, where they are from):

_____

One thing I learned about the world today:

_____

One thing I learned about myself today:

_____

One thing I will do different tomorrow:

_____

General thoughts about today:

_____

_____

_____

DATE: _____   PLACE: _____   BUDGET: _____

"Life is an adventure that is best lived boldly."
— Bear Grylls

3 things I did today:

01. _____

02. _____

03. _____

Favorite thing I ate today:

_____

One person I met today (name, age, where they are from):

_____

One thing I learned about the world today:

_____

One thing I learned about myself today:

_____

One thing I will do different tomorrow:

_____

General thoughts about today:

_____

_____

_____

DATE: _____   **PLACE:** _____   **BUDGET:** _____

---◆---

3 things I did today:

01. _____

02. _____

03. _____

Favorite thing I ate today:

_____

One person I met today (name, age, where they are from):

_____

One thing I learned about the world today:

_____

One thing I learned about myself today:

_____

One thing I will do different tomorrow:

_____

General thoughts about today:

_____

_____

_____

DATE: _____ **PLACE:** _____ **BUDGET:** _____

"Surely, of all the wonders of the world, the horizon is the greatest."
— Freya Stark

3 things I did today:

01. _____

02. _____

03. _____

Favorite thing I ate today:

_____

One person I met today (name, age, where they are from):

_____

One thing I learned about the world today:

_____

One thing I learned about myself today:

_____

One thing I will do different tomorrow:

_____

General thoughts about today:

_____

_____

_____

DATE: _____   **PLACE:** _____   **BUDGET:** _____

———————————✦———————————

3 things I did today:

01. _____

02. _____

03. _____

Favorite thing I ate today:

_____

One person I met today (name, age, where they are from):

_____

One thing I learned about the world today:

_____

One thing I learned about myself today:

_____

One thing I will do different tomorrow:

_____

General thoughts about today:

_____

_____

_____

DATE: _____ **PLACE:** _____ **BUDGET:** _____

"The journey not the arrival matters."
— T.S. Eliot

3 things I did today:

01. _____

02. _____

03. _____

Favorite thing I ate today:

_____

One person I met today (name, age, where they are from):

_____

One thing I learned about the world today:

_____

One thing I learned about myself today:

_____

One thing I will do different tomorrow:

_____

General thoughts about today:

_____

_____

_____

DATE: _____   **PLACE:** _____   **BUDGET:** _____

———————————◈———————————

3 things I did today:

01. _____

02. _____

03. _____

Favorite thing I ate today:

_____

One person I met today (name, age, where they are from):

_____

One thing I learned about the world today:

_____

One thing I learned about myself today:

_____

One thing I will do different tomorrow:

_____

General thoughts about today:

_____

_____

_____

DATE: _____ **PLACE:** _____ **BUDGET:** _____

"I am not born for one corner; the whole world is my native land."
— Seneca

3 things I did today:

01. _____

02. _____

03. _____

Favorite thing I ate today:

_____

One person I met today (name, age, where they are from):

_____

One thing I learned about the world today:

_____

One thing I learned about myself today:

_____

One thing I will do different tomorrow:

_____

General thoughts about today:

_____

_____

_____

DATE: _____ **PLACE:** _____ **BUDGET:** _____

———————————◆———————————

3 things I did today:

01. _____

02. _____

03. _____

Favorite thing I ate today:

_____

One person I met today (name, age, where they are from):

_____

One thing I learned about the world today:

_____

One thing I learned about myself today:

_____

One thing I will do different tomorrow:

_____

General thoughts about today:

_____

_____

_____

DATE: _____ **PLACE:** _____ **BUDGET:** _____

"Your passion is waiting for your courage to catch up."
— Isabelle Lafleche

3 things I did today:

01. _____

02. _____

03. _____

Favorite thing I ate today:

_____

One person I met today (name, age, where they are from):

_____

One thing I learned about the world today:

_____

One thing I learned about myself today:

_____

One thing I will do different tomorrow:

_____

General thoughts about today:

_____

_____

_____

DATE: _____ **PLACE:** _____ **BUDGET:** _____

---------- ✦ ----------

3 things I did today:

01. _____

02. _____

03. _____

Favorite thing I ate today:

_____

One person I met today (name, age, where they are from):

_____

One thing I learned about the world today:

_____

One thing I learned about myself today:

_____

One thing I will do different tomorrow:

_____

General thoughts about today:

_____

_____

_____

"Once you have traveled, the voyage never ends, but is played out over and over again in the quietest chambers. The mind can never break off from the journey." — Pat Conroy

3 things I did today:

01. _____

02. _____

03. _____

Favorite thing I ate today:

_____

One person I met today (name, age, where they are from):

_____

One thing I learned about the world today:

_____

One thing I learned about myself today:

_____

One thing I will do different tomorrow:

_____

General thoughts about today:

_____

_____

_____

DATE: _____   **PLACE:** _____   **BUDGET:** _____

———————————— ✦ ————————————

3 things I did today:

01. _____

02. _____

03. _____

Favorite thing I ate today:

_____

One person I met today (name, age, where they are from):

_____

One thing I learned about the world today:

_____

One thing I learned about myself today:

_____

One thing I will do different tomorrow:

_____

General thoughts about today:

_____

_____

_____

DATE: _____   PLACE: _____   BUDGET: _____

"Take only memories, leave only footprints."
— Chief Seattle

3 things I did today:

01. _____

02. _____

03. _____

Favorite thing I ate today:

_____

One person I met today (name, age, where they are from):

_____

One thing I learned about the world today:

_____

One thing I learned about myself today:

_____

One thing I will do different tomorrow:

_____

General thoughts about today:

_____

_____

_____

DATE: _____   **PLACE:** _____   **BUDGET:** _____

---

3 things I did today:

01. _____

02. _____

03. _____

Favorite thing I ate today:

_____

One person I met today (name, age, where they are from):

_____

One thing I learned about the world today:

_____

One thing I learned about myself today:

_____

One thing I will do different tomorrow:

_____

General thoughts about today:

_____

_____

_____

DATE: _____   **PLACE:** _____   **BUDGET:** _____

"Don't ever live vicariously. This is your life. Live."

— Lavinia Spalding

3 things I did today:

01. _____

02. _____

03. _____

Favorite thing I ate today:

_____

One person I met today (name, age, where they are from):

_____

One thing I learned about the world today:

_____

One thing I learned about myself today:

_____

One thing I will do different tomorrow:

_____

General thoughts about today:

_____

_____

_____

DATE: _____   **PLACE:** _____   **BUDGET:** _____

---------------◆---------------

3 things I did today:

01. _____

02. _____

03. _____

Favorite thing I ate today:

_____

One person I met today (name, age, where they are from):

_____

One thing I learned about the world today:

_____

One thing I learned about myself today:

_____

One thing I will do different tomorrow:

_____

General thoughts about today:

_____

_____

_____

DATE: _____ **PLACE:** _____ **BUDGET:** _____

"Our battered suitcases were piled on the sidewalk again; we had longer ways to go.
But no matter, the road is life." — Jack Kerouac

3 things I did today:

01. _____

02. _____

03. _____

Favorite thing I ate today:

_____

One person I met today (name, age, where they are from):

_____

One thing I learned about the world today:

_____

One thing I learned about myself today:

_____

One thing I will do different tomorrow:

_____

General thoughts about today:

_____

_____

_____

DATE: _____   **PLACE:** _____   **BUDGET:** _____

───────────◆───────────

3 things I did today:

01. _____

02. _____

03. _____

Favorite thing I ate today:

_____

One person I met today (name, age, where they are from):

_____

One thing I learned about the world today:

_____

One thing I learned about myself today:

_____

One thing I will do different tomorrow:

_____

General thoughts about today:

_____

_____

_____

DATE: _____   **PLACE:** _____   **BUDGET:** _____

"Life is a journey with almost limitless detours."
— Ken Poirot

3 things I did today:

01. _____

02. _____

03. _____

Favorite thing I ate today:

_____

One person I met today (name, age, where they are from):

_____

One thing I learned about the world today:

_____

One thing I learned about myself today:

_____

One thing I will do different tomorrow:

_____

General thoughts about today:

_____

_____

_____

DATE: _____ **PLACE:** _____ **BUDGET:** _____

———————————— ✦ ————————————

3 things I did today:

01. _____

02. _____

03. _____

Favorite thing I ate today:

_____

One person I met today (name, age, where they are from):

_____

One thing I learned about the world today:

_____

One thing I learned about myself today:

_____

One thing I will do different tomorrow:

_____

General thoughts about today:

_____

_____

_____

DATE: _____ **PLACE:** _____ **BUDGET:** _____

"Blessed are the curious for they shall have adventures."
— Lovelle Drachman

3 things I did today:

01. _____

02. _____

03. _____

Favorite thing I ate today:

_____

One person I met today (name, age, where they are from):

_____

One thing I learned about the world today:

_____

One thing I learned about myself today:

_____

One thing I will do different tomorrow:

_____

General thoughts about today:

_____

_____

_____

DATE: _____   **PLACE:** _____   **BUDGET:** _____

---

3 things I did today:

01. _____

02. _____

03. _____

Favorite thing I ate today:

_____

One person I met today (name, age, where they are from):

_____

One thing I learned about the world today:

_____

One thing I learned about myself today:

_____

One thing I will do different tomorrow:

_____

General thoughts about today:

_____

_____

_____

DATE: _____   **PLACE:** _____   **BUDGET:** _____

"So much of who we are is where we have been."
— William Langewiesche

3 things I did today:

01. _____

02. _____

03. _____

Favorite thing I ate today:

_____

One person I met today (name, age, where they are from):

_____

One thing I learned about the world today:

_____

One thing I learned about myself today:

_____

One thing I will do different tomorrow:

_____

General thoughts about today:

_____

_____

_____

DATE: _____   **PLACE:** _____   **BUDGET:** _____

---◆---

3 things I did today:

01. _____

02. _____

03. _____

Favorite thing I ate today:

_____

One person I met today (name, age, where they are from):

_____

One thing I learned about the world today:

_____

One thing I learned about myself today:

_____

One thing I will do different tomorrow:

_____

General thoughts about today:

_____

_____

_____

DATE: _____   **PLACE:** _____   **BUDGET:** _____

"Find out how other people live and eat and cook. Learn from them –
wherever you go." — Anthony Bourdain

3 things I did today:

01. _____

02. _____

03. _____

Favorite thing I ate today:

_____

One person I met today (name, age, where they are from):

_____

One thing I learned about the world today:

_____

One thing I learned about myself today:

_____

One thing I will do different tomorrow:

_____

General thoughts about today:

_____

_____

_____

DATE: _____   **PLACE:** _____   **BUDGET:** _____

———————————◆———————————

3 things I did today:

01. _____

02. _____

03. _____

Favorite thing I ate today:

_____

One person I met today (name, age, where they are from):

_____

One thing I learned about the world today:

_____

One thing I learned about myself today:

_____

One thing I will do different tomorrow:

_____

General thoughts about today:

_____

_____

_____

DATE: _____ **PLACE:** _____ **BUDGET:** _____

"Take the time to put the camera away and gaze in wonder at what's there in front of you." — Erick Widman

3 things I did today:

01. _____

02. _____

03. _____

Favorite thing I ate today:

_____

One person I met today (name, age, where they are from):

_____

One thing I learned about the world today:

_____

One thing I learned about myself today:

_____

One thing I will do different tomorrow:

_____

General thoughts about today:

_____

_____

_____

DATE: _____ **PLACE:** _____ **BUDGET:** _____

———————————◆———————————

3 things I did today:

01. _____

02. _____

03. _____

Favorite thing I ate today:

_____

One person I met today (name, age, where they are from):

_____

One thing I learned about the world today:

_____

One thing I learned about myself today:

_____

One thing I will do different tomorrow:

_____

General thoughts about today:

_____

_____

_____

DATE: _____   **PLACE:** _____   **BUDGET:** _____

"Never get so busy making a living that you forget to make a life."
— Dolly Parton

3 things I did today:

01. _____

02. _____

03. _____

Favorite thing I ate today:

_____

One person I met today (name, age, where they are from):

_____

One thing I learned about the world today:

_____

One thing I learned about myself today:

_____

One thing I will do different tomorrow:

_____

General thoughts about today:

_____

_____

_____

DATE: _____   **PLACE:** _____   **BUDGET:** _____

———————————◆———————————

3 things I did today:

01. _____

02. _____

03. _____

Favorite thing I ate today:

_____

One person I met today (name, age, where they are from):

_____

One thing I learned about the world today:

_____

One thing I learned about myself today:

_____

One thing I will do different tomorrow:

_____

General thoughts about today:

_____

_____

_____

"Your assumptions are your windows on the world. Scrub them off every once in a while, or the light won't come in." — Alan Alda

3 things I did today:

01. _____

02. _____

03. _____

Favorite thing I ate today:

_____

One person I met today (name, age, where they are from):

_____

One thing I learned about the world today:

_____

One thing I learned about myself today:

_____

One thing I will do different tomorrow:

_____

General thoughts about today:

_____

_____

_____

DATE: _____   **PLACE:** _____   **BUDGET:** _____

---

3 things I did today:

01. _____

02. _____

03. _____

Favorite thing I ate today:

_____

One person I met today (name, age, where they are from):

_____

One thing I learned about the world today:

_____

One thing I learned about myself today:

_____

One thing I will do different tomorrow:

_____

General thoughts about today:

_____

_____

_____

DATE: _____   **PLACE:** _____   **BUDGET:** _____

"Wherever you go, go with all your heart."
— Confucius

3 things I did today:

01. _____

02. _____

03. _____

Favorite thing I ate today:

_____

One person I met today (name, age, where they are from):

_____

One thing I learned about the world today:

_____

One thing I learned about myself today:

_____

One thing I will do different tomorrow:

_____

General thoughts about today:

_____

_____

_____

————————◈————————

3 things I did today:

01. _____

02. _____

03. _____

Favorite thing I ate today:

_____

One person I met today (name, age, where they are from):

_____

One thing I learned about the world today:

_____

One thing I learned about myself today:

_____

One thing I will do different tomorrow:

_____

General thoughts about today:

_____

_____

_____

DATE: _____ **PLACE:** _____ **BUDGET:** _____

"He who does not travel does not know the value of men."
— Moorish Proverb

3 things I did today:

01. _____

02. _____

03. _____

Favorite thing I ate today:

_____

One person I met today (name, age, where they are from):

_____

One thing I learned about the world today:

_____

One thing I learned about myself today:

_____

One thing I will do different tomorrow:

_____

General thoughts about today:

_____

_____

_____

DATE: _____   **PLACE:** _____   **BUDGET:** _____

---

3 things I did today:

01. _____

02. _____

03. _____

Favorite thing I ate today:

_____

One person I met today (name, age, where they are from):

_____

One thing I learned about the world today:

_____

One thing I learned about myself today:

_____

One thing I will do different tomorrow:

_____

General thoughts about today:

_____

_____

_____

DATE: _____   **PLACE:** _____   **BUDGET:** _____

"Just don't give up what you're trying to do. Where there is love and inspiration, I don't think you can go wrong." — Ella Fitzgerald

3 things I did today:

01. _____

02. _____

03. _____

Favorite thing I ate today:

_____

One person I met today (name, age, where they are from):

_____

One thing I learned about the world today:

_____

One thing I learned about myself today:

_____

One thing I will do different tomorrow:

_____

General thoughts about today:

_____

_____

_____

DATE: _____ **PLACE:** _____ **BUDGET:** _____

--- ✦ ---

3 things I did today:

01. _____

02. _____

03. _____

Favorite thing I ate today:

_____

One person I met today (name, age, where they are from):

_____

One thing I learned about the world today:

_____

One thing I learned about myself today:

_____

One thing I will do different tomorrow:

_____

General thoughts about today:

_____

_____

_____

"No place is ever as bad as they tell you it's going to be."

— Chuck Thompson

3 things I did today:

01. _____

02. _____

03. _____

Favorite thing I ate today:

_____

One person I met today (name, age, where they are from):

_____

One thing I learned about the world today:

_____

One thing I learned about myself today:

_____

One thing I will do different tomorrow:

_____

General thoughts about today:

_____

_____

_____

DATE: _____ **PLACE:** _____ **BUDGET:** _____

————————◈————————

3 things I did today:

01. _____ _____

02. _____

03. _____

Favorite thing I ate today:

_____

One person I met today (name, age, where they are from):

_____

One thing I learned about the world today:

_____

One thing I learned about myself today:

_____

One thing I will do different tomorrow:

_____

General thoughts about today:

_____

_____

_____

"If you don't like the road you're walking, start paving another one."
— Dolly Parton

3 things I did today:

01. _____

02. _____

03. _____

Favorite thing I ate today:

_____

One person I met today (name, age, where they are from):

_____

One thing I learned about the world today:

_____

One thing I learned about myself today:

_____

One thing I will do different tomorrow:

_____

General thoughts about today:

_____

_____

_____

DATE: _____ **PLACE:** _____ **BUDGET:** _____

———————◈———————

3 things I did today:

01. _____ _____

02. _____

03. _____

Favorite thing I ate today:

_____

One person I met today (name, age, where they are from):

_____

One thing I learned about the world today:

_____

One thing I learned about myself today:

_____

One thing I will do different tomorrow:

_____

General thoughts about today:

_____

_____

_____

DATE: _____ **PLACE:** _____ **BUDGET:** _____

"Do you really want to look back on your life and see how wonderful it could have been had you not been afraid to live it?" — Caroline Myss

3 things I did today:

01. _____

02. _____

03. _____

Favorite thing I ate today:

_____

One person I met today (name, age, where they are from):

_____

One thing I learned about the world today:

_____

One thing I learned about myself today:

_____

One thing I will do different tomorrow:

_____

General thoughts about today:

_____

_____

_____

DATE: _____   **PLACE:** _____   **BUDGET:** _____

———————————◈———————————

3 things I did today:

01. _____

02. _____

03. _____

Favorite thing I ate today:

_____

One person I met today (name, age, where they are from):

_____

One thing I learned about the world today:

_____

One thing I learned about myself today:

_____

One thing I will do different tomorrow:

_____

General thoughts about today:

_____

_____

_____

"To live is the rarest thing in the world. Most people just exist."
— Oscar Wilde

3 things I did today:

01. _____

02. _____

03. _____

Favorite thing I ate today:

_____

One person I met today (name, age, where they are from):

_____

One thing I learned about the world today:

_____

One thing I learned about myself today:

_____

One thing I will do different tomorrow:

_____

General thoughts about today:

_____

_____

_____

DATE: _____ **PLACE:** _____ **BUDGET:** _____

———————— ✦ ————————

3 things I did today:

01. _____

02. _____

03. _____

Favorite thing I ate today:

_____

One person I met today (name, age, where they are from):

_____

One thing I learned about the world today:

_____

One thing I learned about myself today:

_____

One thing I will do different tomorrow:

_____

General thoughts about today:

_____

_____

_____

DATE: _____   PLACE: _____   BUDGET: _____

"There is no moment of delight in any pilgrimage like the beginning of it."
— Charles Dudley Warner

3 things I did today:

01. _____

02. _____

03. _____

Favorite thing I ate today:

_____

One person I met today (name, age, where they are from):

_____

One thing I learned about the world today:

_____

One thing I learned about myself today:

_____

One thing I will do different tomorrow:

_____

General thoughts about today:

_____

_____

_____

DATE: _____   **PLACE:** _____   **BUDGET:** _____

---

3 things I did today:

01. _____

02. _____

03. _____

Favorite thing I ate today:

_____

One person I met today (name, age, where they are from):

_____

One thing I learned about the world today:

_____

One thing I learned about myself today:

_____

One thing I will do different tomorrow:

_____

General thoughts about today:

_____

_____

_____

DATE: _____   **PLACE:** _____   **BUDGET:** _____

"Every exit is an entry somewhere else."
— Tom Stoppard

3 things I did today:

01. _____

02. _____

03. _____

Favorite thing I ate today:

_____

One person I met today (name, age, where they are from):

_____

One thing I learned about the world today:

_____

One thing I learned about myself today:

_____

One thing I will do different tomorrow:

_____

General thoughts about today:

_____

_____

_____

DATE: _____   **PLACE:** _____   **BUDGET:** _____

——————————◆——————————

3 things I did today:

01. _____

02. _____

03. _____

Favorite thing I ate today:

_____

One person I met today (name, age, where they are from):

_____

One thing I learned about the world today:

_____

One thing I learned about myself today:

_____

One thing I will do different tomorrow:

_____

General thoughts about today:

_____

_____

_____

DATE: _____   **PLACE:** _____   **BUDGET:** _____

"There are only two emotions in a plane: boredom and terror."
— Orson Welles

3 things I did today:

01. _____

02. _____

03. _____

Favorite thing I ate today:

_____

One person I met today (name, age, where they are from):

_____

One thing I learned about the world today:

_____

One thing I learned about myself today:

_____

One thing I will do different tomorrow:

_____

General thoughts about today:

_____

_____

_____

DATE: _____ **PLACE:** _____ **BUDGET:** _____

───────────────◆───────────────

3 things I did today:

01. _____

02. _____

03. _____

Favorite thing I ate today:

_____

One person I met today (name, age, where they are from):

_____

One thing I learned about the world today:

_____

One thing I learned about myself today:

_____

One thing I will do different tomorrow:

_____

General thoughts about today:

_____

_____

_____

DATE: _____   **PLACE:** _____   **BUDGET:** _____

"Travel is as much a passion as ambition or love."
— Letitia Elizabeth Landon

3 things I did today:

01. _____

02. _____

03. _____

Favorite thing I ate today:

_____

One person I met today (name, age, where they are from):

_____

One thing I learned about the world today:

_____

One thing I learned about myself today:

_____

One thing I will do different tomorrow:

_____

General thoughts about today:

_____

_____

_____

DATE: _____   **PLACE:** _____   **BUDGET:** _____

--------------◈--------------

3 things I did today:

01. _____

02. _____

03. _____

Favorite thing I ate today:

_____

One person I met today (name, age, where they are from):

_____

One thing I learned about the world today:

_____

One thing I learned about myself today:

_____

One thing I will do different tomorrow:

_____

General thoughts about today:

_____

_____

_____

DATE: _____ **PLACE:** _____ **BUDGET:** _____

"Impossible is just an opinion."
— Paulo Coelho

3 things I did today:

01. _____

02. _____

03. _____

Favorite thing I ate today:

_____

One person I met today (name, age, where they are from):

_____

One thing I learned about the world today:

_____

One thing I learned about myself today:

_____

One thing I will do different tomorrow:

_____

General thoughts about today:

_____

_____

_____

DATE: _____ **PLACE:** _____ **BUDGET:** _____

———————————— ✦ ————————————

3 things I did today:

01. _____

02. _____

03. _____

Favorite thing I ate today:

_____

One person I met today (name, age, where they are from):

_____

One thing I learned about the world today:

_____

One thing I learned about myself today:

_____

One thing I will do different tomorrow:

_____

General thoughts about today:

_____

_____

_____

DATE: _____   **PLACE:** _____   **BUDGET:** _____

"We travel, some of us forever, to seek other states, other lives, other souls."
— Anaïs Nin

3 things I did today:

01. _____

02. _____

03. _____

Favorite thing I ate today:

_____

One person I met today (name, age, where they are from):

_____

One thing I learned about the world today:

_____

One thing I learned about myself today:

_____

One thing I will do different tomorrow:

_____

General thoughts about today:

_____

_____

_____

DATE: _____   **PLACE:** _____   **BUDGET:** _____

———————————— ✦ ————————————

3 things I did today:

01. _____

02. _____

03. _____

Favorite thing I ate today:

_____

One person I met today (name, age, where they are from):

_____

One thing I learned about the world today:

_____

One thing I learned about myself today:

_____

One thing I will do different tomorrow:

_____

General thoughts about today:

_____

_____

_____

DATE: _____ **PLACE:** _____ **BUDGET:** _____

"We travel, initially, to lose ourselves; and we travel, next to find ourselves."
— Pico Iyer

3 things I did today:

01. _____

02. _____

03. _____

Favorite thing I ate today:

_____

One person I met today (name, age, where they are from):

_____

One thing I learned about the world today:

_____

One thing I learned about myself today:

_____

One thing I will do different tomorrow:

_____

General thoughts about today:

_____

_____

_____

DATE: _____ **PLACE:** _____ **BUDGET:** _____

————————— ✦ —————————

3 things I did today:

01. _____

02. _____

03. _____

Favorite thing I ate today:

_____

One person I met today (name, age, where they are from):

_____

One thing I learned about the world today:

_____

One thing I learned about myself today:

_____

One thing I will do different tomorrow:

_____

General thoughts about today:

_____

_____

_____

DATE: _____   **PLACE:** _____   **BUDGET:** _____

"Traveling – it leaves you speechless, then turns you into a storyteller."

— Ibn Battuta

3 things I did today:

01. _____

02. _____

03. _____

Favorite thing I ate today:

_____

One person I met today (name, age, where they are from):

_____

One thing I learned about the world today:

_____

One thing I learned about myself today:

_____

One thing I will do different tomorrow:

_____

General thoughts about today:

_____

_____

_____

3 things I did today:

01. _____

02. _____

03. _____

Favorite thing I ate today:

_____

One person I met today (name, age, where they are from):

_____

One thing I learned about the world today:

_____

One thing I learned about myself today:

_____

One thing I will do different tomorrow:

_____

General thoughts about today:

_____

_____

_____

"Life's under no obligation to give us what we expect."
— Margaret Mitchell

3 things I did today:

01. _____

02. _____

03. _____

Favorite thing I ate today:

_____

One person I met today (name, age, where they are from):

_____

One thing I learned about the world today:

_____

One thing I learned about myself today:

_____

One thing I will do different tomorrow:

_____

General thoughts about today:

_____

_____

_____

DATE: _____ **PLACE:** _____ **BUDGET:** _____

———————— ✦ ————————

3 things I did today:

01. _____

02. _____

03. _____

Favorite thing I ate today:

_____

One person I met today (name, age, where they are from):

_____

One thing I learned about the world today:

_____

One thing I learned about myself today:

_____

One thing I will do different tomorrow:

_____

General thoughts about today:

_____

_____

_____

DATE: _____ **PLACE:** _____ **BUDGET:** _____

"Remember that happiness is a way of travel – not a destination."
— Roy M. Goodman

3 things I did today:

01. _____

02. _____

03. _____

Favorite thing I ate today:

_____

One person I met today (name, age, where they are from):

_____

One thing I learned about the world today:

_____

One thing I learned about myself today:

_____

One thing I will do different tomorrow:

_____

General thoughts about today:

_____

_____

_____

DATE: _____ **PLACE:** _____ **BUDGET:** _____

---✦---

3 things I did today:

01. _____

02. _____

03. _____

Favorite thing I ate today:

_____

One person I met today (name, age, where they are from):

_____

One thing I learned about the world today:

_____

One thing I learned about myself today:

_____

One thing I will do different tomorrow:

_____

General thoughts about today:

_____

_____

_____

DATE: _____ **PLACE:** _____ **BUDGET:** _____

"Travel doesn't become adventure until you leave yourself behind."
— Marty Rubin

3 things I did today:

01. _____

02. _____

03. _____

Favorite thing I ate today:

_____

One person I met today (name, age, where they are from):

_____

One thing I learned about the world today:

_____

One thing I learned about myself today:

_____

One thing I will do different tomorrow:

_____

General thoughts about today:

_____

_____

_____

DATE: _____ **PLACE:** _____ **BUDGET:** _____

———————— ✦ ————————

3 things I did today:

01. _____

02. _____

03. _____

Favorite thing I ate today:

_____

One person I met today (name, age, where they are from):

_____

One thing I learned about the world today:

_____

One thing I learned about myself today:

_____

One thing I will do different tomorrow:

_____

General thoughts about today:

_____

_____

_____

DATE: _____   PLACE: _____   BUDGET: _____

"Man cannot discover new oceans unless he has the courage to lose sight
of the shore." — Andre Gide

3 things I did today:

01. _____

02. _____

03. _____

Favorite thing I ate today:

_____

One person I met today (name, age, where they are from):

_____

One thing I learned about the world today:

_____

One thing I learned about myself today:

_____

One thing I will do different tomorrow:

_____

General thoughts about today:

_____

_____

_____

DATE: _____   **PLACE:** _____   **BUDGET:** _____

———————◆———————

3 things I did today:

01. _____

02. _____

03. _____

Favorite thing I ate today:

_____

One person I met today (name, age, where they are from):

_____

One thing I learned about the world today:

_____

One thing I learned about myself today:

_____

One thing I will do different tomorrow:

_____

General thoughts about today:

_____

_____

_____

DATE: _____   **PLACE:** _____   **BUDGET:** _____

"Life is a blank canvas, and you need to throw all the paint on it you can."
— Danny Kaye

3 things I did today:

01. _____

02. _____

03. _____

Favorite thing I ate today:

_____

One person I met today (name, age, where they are from):

_____

One thing I learned about the world today:

_____

One thing I learned about myself today:

_____

One thing I will do different tomorrow:

_____

General thoughts about today:

_____

_____

_____

DATE: _____ **PLACE:** _____ **BUDGET:** _____

---◆---

3 things I did today:

01. _____

02. _____

03. _____

Favorite thing I ate today:

_____

One person I met today (name, age, where they are from):

_____

One thing I learned about the world today:

_____

One thing I learned about myself today:

_____

One thing I will do different tomorrow:

_____

General thoughts about today:

_____

_____

_____

DATE: _____   **PLACE:** _____   **BUDGET:** _____

"A traveler without observation is a bird without wings."
— Moslih Eddin Saadi

3 things I did today:

01. _____

02. _____

03. _____

Favorite thing I ate today:

_____

One person I met today (name, age, where they are from):

_____

One thing I learned about the world today:

_____

One thing I learned about myself today:

_____

One thing I will do different tomorrow:

_____

General thoughts about today:

_____

_____

_____

3 things I did today:

01. _____

02. _____

03. _____

Favorite thing I ate today:

_____

One person I met today (name, age, where they are from):

_____

One thing I learned about the world today:

_____

One thing I learned about myself today:

_____

One thing I will do different tomorrow:

_____

General thoughts about today:

_____

_____

_____

DATE: _____   **PLACE:** _____   **BUDGET:** _____

"With age, comes wisdom. With travel, comes understanding."
— Sandra Lake

3 things I did today:

01. _____

02. _____

03. _____

Favorite thing I ate today:

_____

One person I met today (name, age, where they are from):

_____

One thing I learned about the world today:

_____

One thing I learned about myself today:

_____

One thing I will do different tomorrow:

_____

General thoughts about today:

_____

_____

_____

DATE: _____   **PLACE:** _____   **BUDGET:** _____

---

3 things I did today:

01. _____

02. _____

03. _____

Favorite thing I ate today:

_____

One person I met today (name, age, where they are from):

_____

One thing I learned about the world today:

_____

One thing I learned about myself today:

_____

One thing I will do different tomorrow:

_____

General thoughts about today:

_____

_____

_____

DATE: _____ **PLACE:** _____ **BUDGET:** _____

"The world is full of nice people. If you can't find one, be one."

— Nishan Panwar

3 things I did today:

01. _____

02. _____

03. _____

Favorite thing I ate today:

_____

One person I met today (name, age, where they are from):

_____

One thing I learned about the world today:

_____

One thing I learned about myself today:

_____

One thing I will do different tomorrow:

_____

General thoughts about today:

_____

_____

_____

DATE: _____ **PLACE:** _____ **BUDGET:** _____

———————————✦———————————

3 things I did today:

01. _____

02. _____

03. _____

Favorite thing I ate today:

_____

One person I met today (name, age, where they are from):

_____

One thing I learned about the world today:

_____

One thing I learned about myself today:

_____

One thing I will do different tomorrow:

_____

General thoughts about today:

_____

_____

_____

DATE: _____   **PLACE:** _____   **BUDGET:** _____

"You can't go back and change the beginning, but you can start where you are and change the ending." — Unknown

3 things I did today:

01. _____

02. _____

03. _____

Favorite thing I ate today:

_____

One person I met today (name, age, where they are from):

_____

One thing I learned about the world today:

_____

One thing I learned about myself today:

_____

One thing I will do different tomorrow:

_____

General thoughts about today:

_____

_____

_____

DATE: _____ **PLACE:** _____ **BUDGET:** _____

---✦---

3 things I did today:

01. _____

02. _____

03. _____

Favorite thing I ate today:

_____

One person I met today (name, age, where they are from):

_____

One thing I learned about the world today:

_____

One thing I learned about myself today:

_____

One thing I will do different tomorrow:

_____

General thoughts about today:

_____

_____

_____

DATE: _____   **PLACE:** _____   **BUDGET:** _____

"Own only what you can always carry with you: known languages, known countries, known people. Let your memory be your travel bag." — Alexandr Solzhenit

3 things I did today:

01. _____

02. _____

03. _____

Favorite thing I ate today:

_____

One person I met today (name, age, where they are from):

_____

One thing I learned about the world today:

_____

One thing I learned about myself today:

_____

One thing I will do different tomorrow:

_____

General thoughts about today:

_____

_____

_____

DATE: _____   **PLACE:** _____   **BUDGET:** _____

---------------◆---------------

3 things I did today:

01. _____

02. _____

03. _____

Favorite thing I ate today:

_____

One person I met today (name, age, where they are from):

_____

One thing I learned about the world today:

_____

One thing I learned about myself today:

_____

One thing I will do different tomorrow:

_____

General thoughts about today:

_____

_____

_____

DATE: _____   **PLACE:** _____   **BUDGET:** _____

"Travelling tends to magnify all human emotions."
— Peter Hoeg

3 things I did today:

01. _____

02. _____

03. _____

Favorite thing I ate today:

_____

One person I met today (name, age, where they are from):

_____

One thing I learned about the world today:

_____

One thing I learned about myself today:

_____

One thing I will do different tomorrow:

_____

General thoughts about today:

_____

_____

_____

DATE: _____ **PLACE:** _____ **BUDGET:** _____

---◆---

3 things I did today:

01. _____

02. _____

03. _____

Favorite thing I ate today:

_____

One person I met today (name, age, where they are from):

_____

One thing I learned about the world today:

_____

One thing I learned about myself today:

_____

One thing I will do different tomorrow:

_____

General thoughts about today:

_____

_____

_____

"Travel makes a wise man better but a fool worse."
— Thomas Fuller

3 things I did today:

01. _____

02. _____

03. _____

Favorite thing I ate today:

_____

One person I met today (name, age, where they are from):

_____

One thing I learned about the world today:

_____

One thing I learned about myself today:

_____

One thing I will do different tomorrow:

_____

General thoughts about today:

_____

_____

_____

DATE: _____   **PLACE:** _____   **BUDGET:** _____

---- ✦ ----

3 things I did today:

01. _____

02. _____

03. _____

Favorite thing I ate today:

_____

One person I met today (name, age, where they are from):

_____

One thing I learned about the world today:

_____

One thing I learned about myself today:

_____

One thing I will do different tomorrow:

_____

General thoughts about today:

_____

_____

_____

"No man ever steps in the same river twice, for it's not the same river and he's not the same man." — Heraclitus

3 things I did today:

01. _____

02. _____

03. _____

Favorite thing I ate today:

_____

One person I met today (name, age, where they are from):

_____

One thing I learned about the world today:

_____

One thing I learned about myself today:

_____

One thing I will do different tomorrow:

_____

General thoughts about today:

_____

_____

_____

DATE: _____ **PLACE:** _____ **BUDGET:** _____

———————◆———————

3 things I did today:

01. _____

02. _____

03. _____

Favorite thing I ate today:

_____

One person I met today (name, age, where they are from):

_____

One thing I learned about the world today:

_____

One thing I learned about myself today:

_____

One thing I will do different tomorrow:

_____

General thoughts about today:

_____

_____

_____

DATE: _____   **PLACE:** _____   **BUDGET:** _____

"I travel because it makes me realize how much I haven't seen, how much I'm not going to see, and how much I still need to see." — Carew Papritz

3 things I did today:

01. _____

02. _____

03. _____

Favorite thing I ate today:

_____

One person I met today (name, age, where they are from):

_____

One thing I learned about the world today:

_____

One thing I learned about myself today:

_____

One thing I will do different tomorrow:

_____

General thoughts about today:

_____

_____

_____

DATE: _____   **PLACE:** _____   **BUDGET:** _____

———————————◆———————————

3 things I did today:

01. _____

02. _____

03. _____

Favorite thing I ate today:

_____

One person I met today (name, age, where they are from):

_____

One thing I learned about the world today:

_____

One thing I learned about myself today:

_____

One thing I will do different tomorrow:

_____

General thoughts about today:

_____

_____

_____

DATE: _____ PLACE: _____ BUDGET: _____

"Once in a while it really hits people that they don't have to experience the world in the way they have been told to." — Alan Keightley

3 things I did today:

01. _____

02. _____

03. _____

Favorite thing I ate today:

_____

One person I met today (name, age, where they are from):

_____

One thing I learned about the world today:

_____

One thing I learned about myself today:

_____

One thing I will do different tomorrow:

_____

General thoughts about today:

_____

_____

_____

DATE: _____ **PLACE:** _____ **BUDGET:** _____

———————————◆———————————

3 things I did today:

01. _____

02. _____

03. _____

Favorite thing I ate today:

_____

One person I met today (name, age, where they are from):

_____

One thing I learned about the world today:

_____

One thing I learned about myself today:

_____

One thing I will do different tomorrow:

_____

General thoughts about today:

_____

_____

_____

DATE: _____   PLACE: _____   BUDGET: _____

"If opportunity doesn't knock, build a door."
— Milton Berle

3 things I did today:

01. _____

02. _____

03. _____

Favorite thing I ate today:

_____

One person I met today (name, age, where they are from):

_____

One thing I learned about the world today:

_____

One thing I learned about myself today:

_____

One thing I will do different tomorrow:

_____

General thoughts about today:

_____

_____

_____

DATE: _____   **PLACE:** _____   **BUDGET:** _____

---◆---

3 things I did today:

01. _____

02. _____

03. _____

Favorite thing I ate today:

_____

One person I met today (name, age, where they are from):

_____

One thing I learned about the world today:

_____

One thing I learned about myself today:

_____

One thing I will do different tomorrow:

_____

General thoughts about today:

_____

_____

_____

DATE: _____ **PLACE:** _____ **BUDGET:** _____

"Adventure can be an end in itself. Self-discovery is the secret ingredient."
— Grace Lichtenstein

3 things I did today:

01. _____

02. _____

03. _____

Favorite thing I ate today:

_____

One person I met today (name, age, where they are from):

_____

One thing I learned about the world today:

_____

One thing I learned about myself today:

_____

One thing I will do different tomorrow:

_____

General thoughts about today:

_____

_____

_____

DATE: _____ **PLACE:** _____ **BUDGET:** _____

3 things I did today:

01. _____

02. _____

03. _____

Favorite thing I ate today:

_____

One person I met today (name, age, where they are from):

_____

One thing I learned about the world today:

_____

One thing I learned about myself today:

_____

One thing I will do different tomorrow:

_____

General thoughts about today:

_____

_____

_____

DATE: _____   **PLACE:** _____   **BUDGET:** _____

"Don't forget: Beautiful sunsets need cloudy skies."
— Paulo Coelho

3 things I did today:

01. _____

02. _____

03. _____

Favorite thing I ate today:

_____

One person I met today (name, age, where they are from):

_____

One thing I learned about the world today:

_____

One thing I learned about myself today:

_____

One thing I will do different tomorrow:

_____

General thoughts about today:

_____

_____

_____

DATE: _____   **PLACE:** _____   **BUDGET:** _____

————————◆————————

3 things I did today:

01. _____

02. _____

03. _____

Favorite thing I ate today:

_____

One person I met today (name, age, where they are from):

_____

One thing I learned about the world today:

_____

One thing I learned about myself today:

_____

One thing I will do different tomorrow:

_____

General thoughts about today:

_____

_____

_____

"He who would travel happily must travel light."
— Antoine de St. Exupery

3 things I did today:

01. _____

02. _____

03. _____

Favorite thing I ate today:

_____

One person I met today (name, age, where they are from):

_____

One thing I learned about the world today:

_____

One thing I learned about myself today:

_____

One thing I will do different tomorrow:

_____

General thoughts about today:

_____

_____

_____

DATE: _____ **PLACE:** _____ **BUDGET:** _____

———————————————◆———————————————

3 things I did today:

01. _____

02. _____

03. _____

Favorite thing I ate today:

_____

One person I met today (name, age, where they are from):

_____

One thing I learned about the world today:

_____

One thing I learned about myself today:

_____

One thing I will do different tomorrow:

_____

General thoughts about today:

_____

_____

_____

DATE: _____ PLACE: _____ BUDGET: _____

"I am thankful for all of those who said NO to me. It's because of them I'm
doing it myself." — Albert Einstein

3 things I did today:

01. _____

02. _____

03. _____

Favorite thing I ate today:

_____

One person I met today (name, age, where they are from):

_____

One thing I learned about the world today:

_____

One thing I learned about myself today:

_____

One thing I will do different tomorrow:

_____

General thoughts about today:

_____

_____

_____

DATE: _____   **PLACE:** _____   **BUDGET:** _____

─────────────── ✦ ───────────────

3 things I did today:

01. _____

02. _____

03. _____

Favorite thing I ate today:

_____

One person I met today (name, age, where they are from):

_____

One thing I learned about the world today:

_____

One thing I learned about myself today:

_____

One thing I will do different tomorrow:

_____

General thoughts about today:

_____

_____

_____

DATE: _____ **PLACE:** _____ **BUDGET:** _____

"The difference between an adventure and an ordeal is attitude."
— Bob Bitchin

3 things I did today:

01. _____

02. _____

03. _____

Favorite thing I ate today:

_____

One person I met today (name, age, where they are from):

_____

One thing I learned about the world today:

_____

One thing I learned about myself today:

_____

One thing I will do different tomorrow:

_____

General thoughts about today:

_____

_____

_____

DATE: _____ **PLACE:** _____ **BUDGET:** _____

———————— ✦ ————————

3 things I did today:

01. _____

02. _____

03. _____

Favorite thing I ate today:

_____

One person I met today (name, age, where they are from):

_____

One thing I learned about the world today:

_____

One thing I learned about myself today:

_____

One thing I will do different tomorrow:

_____

General thoughts about today:

_____

_____

_____

DATE: _____   PLACE: _____   BUDGET: _____

"Learn to be indifferent to what makes no difference."
— Marcus Aurelius

3 things I did today:

01. _____

02. _____

03. _____

Favorite thing I ate today:

_____

One person I met today (name, age, where they are from):

_____

One thing I learned about the world today:

_____

One thing I learned about myself today:

_____

One thing I will do different tomorrow:

_____

General thoughts about today:

_____

_____

_____

DATE: _____   **PLACE:** _____   **BUDGET:** _____

———————————◆———————————

3 things I did today:

01. _____

02. _____

03. _____

Favorite thing I ate today:

_____

One person I met today (name, age, where they are from):

_____

One thing I learned about the world today:

_____

One thing I learned about myself today:

_____

One thing I will do different tomorrow:

_____

General thoughts about today:

_____

_____

_____

DATE: _____   **PLACE:** _____   **BUDGET:** _____

"Solo travel not only pushes you out of your comfort zone, it also pushes you out of the zone of other's expectations." — Suzy Strutner

3 things I did today:

01. _____

02. _____

03. _____

Favorite thing I ate today:

_____

One person I met today (name, age, where they are from):

_____

One thing I learned about the world today:

_____

One thing I learned about myself today:

_____

One thing I will do different tomorrow:

_____

General thoughts about today:

_____

_____

_____

DATE: _____ **PLACE:** _____ **BUDGET:** _____

——————————— ✦ ———————————

3 things I did today:

01. _____

02. _____

03. _____

Favorite thing I ate today:

_____

One person I met today (name, age, where they are from):

_____

One thing I learned about the world today:

_____

One thing I learned about myself today:

_____

One thing I will do different tomorrow:

_____

General thoughts about today:

_____

_____

_____

DATE: _____   **PLACE:** _____   **BUDGET:** _____

"Stop worrying about the potholes in the road and enjoy the trip."
— Babs Hoffman

3 things I did today:

01. _____

02. _____

03. _____

Favorite thing I ate today:

_____

One person I met today (name, age, where they are from):

_____

One thing I learned about the world today:

_____

One thing I learned about myself today:

_____

One thing I will do different tomorrow:

_____

General thoughts about today:

_____

_____

_____

DATE: _____   **PLACE:** _____   **BUDGET:** _____

---

3 things I did today:

01. _____

02. _____

03. _____

Favorite thing I ate today:

_____

One person I met today (name, age, where they are from):

_____

One thing I learned about the world today:

_____

One thing I learned about myself today:

_____

One thing I will do different tomorrow:

_____

General thoughts about today:

_____

_____

_____

DATE: _____ **PLACE:** _____ **BUDGET:** _____

"The best trips, like the best love affairs, never really end."
— Pico Iyer   .

3 things I did today:

01. _____ _____

02. _____

03. _____

Favorite thing I ate today:

_____

One person I met today (name, age, where they are from):

_____

One thing I learned about the world today:

_____

One thing I learned about myself today:

_____

One thing I will do different tomorrow:

_____

General thoughts about today:

_____

_____

_____

DATE: _____ **PLACE:** _____ **BUDGET:** _____

———————————✦———————————

3 things I did today:

01. _____

02. _____

03. _____

Favorite thing I ate today:

_____

One person I met today (name, age, where they are from):

_____

One thing I learned about the world today:

_____

One thing I learned about myself today:

_____

One thing I will do different tomorrow:

_____

General thoughts about today:

_____

_____

_____

DATE: _____   PLACE: _____   BUDGET: _____

"At its best, travel should challenge our preconceptions and most cherished views."
— Arthur Frommer

3 things I did today:

01. _____

02. _____

03. _____

Favorite thing I ate today:

_____

One person I met today (name, age, where they are from):

_____

One thing I learned about the world today:

_____

One thing I learned about myself today:

_____

One thing I will do different tomorrow:

_____

General thoughts about today:

_____

_____

_____

———————— ✦ ————————

3 things I did today:

01. _____

02. _____

03. _____

Favorite thing I ate today:

_____

One person I met today (name, age, where they are from):

_____

One thing I learned about the world today:

_____

One thing I learned about myself today:

_____

One thing I will do different tomorrow:

_____

General thoughts about today:

_____

_____

_____

DATE: _____   PLACE: _____   BUDGET: _____

"I am not the same, having seen the moon shine on the other side of the world."
— Mary Anne Radmacher

3 things I did today:

01. _____

02. _____

03. _____

Favorite thing I ate today:

_____

One person I met today (name, age, where they are from):

_____

One thing I learned about the world today:

_____

One thing I learned about myself today:

_____

One thing I will do different tomorrow:

_____

General thoughts about today:

_____

_____

_____

DATE: _____   **PLACE:** _____   **BUDGET:** _____

———————————— ✦ ————————————

3 things I did today:

01. _____

02. _____

03. _____

Favorite thing I ate today:

_____

One person I met today (name, age, where they are from):

_____

One thing I learned about the world today:

_____

One thing I learned about myself today:

_____

One thing I will do different tomorrow:

_____

General thoughts about today:

_____

_____

_____

DATE: _____   **PLACE:** _____   **BUDGET:** _____

"Live life with no excuses, travel with no regret."
— Oscar Wilde

3 things I did today:

01. _____ _____

02. _____

03. _____

Favorite thing I ate today:

_____

One person I met today (name, age, where they are from):

_____

One thing I learned about the world today:

_____

One thing I learned about myself today:

_____

One thing I will do different tomorrow:

_____

General thoughts about today:

_____

_____

_____

DATE: _____   **PLACE:** _____   **BUDGET:** _____

———————————◈———————————

3 things I did today:

01. _____

02. _____

03. _____

Favorite thing I ate today:

_____

One person I met today (name, age, where they are from):

_____

One thing I learned about the world today:

_____

One thing I learned about myself today:

_____

One thing I will do different tomorrow:

_____

General thoughts about today:

_____

_____

_____

DATE: _____   PLACE: _____   BUDGET: _____

"How often I found where I should be going only by setting out for somewhere else." — R. Buckminster Fuller

3 things I did today:

01. _____

02. _____

03. _____

Favorite thing I ate today:

_____

One person I met today (name, age, where they are from):

_____

One thing I learned about the world today:

_____

One thing I learned about myself today:

_____

One thing I will do different tomorrow:

_____

General thoughts about today:

_____

_____

_____

DATE: _____   **PLACE:** _____   **BUDGET:** _____

---◆---

3 things I did today:

01. _____

02. _____

03. _____

Favorite thing I ate today:

_____

One person I met today (name, age, where they are from):

_____

One thing I learned about the world today:

_____

One thing I learned about myself today:

_____

One thing I will do different tomorrow:

_____

General thoughts about today:

_____

_____

_____

DATE: _____ **PLACE:** _____ **BUDGET:** _____

"To travel is to discover that everyone is wrong about other countries."
— Aldous Huxley

3 things I did today:

01. _____

02. _____

03. _____

Favorite thing I ate today:

_____

One person I met today (name, age, where they are from):

_____

One thing I learned about the world today:

_____

One thing I learned about myself today:

_____

One thing I will do different tomorrow:

_____

General thoughts about today:

_____

_____

_____

DATE: _____ **PLACE:** _____ **BUDGET:** _____

---◆---

3 things I did today:

01. _____

02. _____

03. _____

Favorite thing I ate today:

_____

One person I met today (name, age, where they are from):

_____

One thing I learned about the world today:

_____

One thing I learned about myself today:

_____

One thing I will do different tomorrow:

_____

General thoughts about today:

_____

_____

_____

"Do not let the behavior of others destroy your inner peace."
— Dalai Lama

3 things I did today:

01. _____ _____

02. _____

03. _____

Favorite thing I ate today:

_____

One person I met today (name, age, where they are from):

_____

One thing I learned about the world today:

_____

One thing I learned about myself today:

_____

One thing I will do different tomorrow:

_____

General thoughts about today:

_____

_____

_____

DATE: _____ **PLACE:** _____ **BUDGET:** _____

———————————— ✦ ————————————

3 things I did today:

01. _____

02. _____

03. _____

Favorite thing I ate today:

_____

One person I met today (name, age, where they are from):

_____

One thing I learned about the world today:

_____

One thing I learned about myself today:

_____

One thing I will do different tomorrow:

_____

General thoughts about today:

_____

_____

_____

DATE: _____   **PLACE:** _____   **BUDGET:** _____

"It's no use going back to yesterday, because I was a different person then."
— Lewis Carroll

3 things I did today:

01. _____

02. _____

03. _____

Favorite thing I ate today:

_____

One person I met today (name, age, where they are from):

_____

One thing I learned about the world today:

_____

One thing I learned about myself today:

_____

One thing I will do different tomorrow:

_____

General thoughts about today:

_____

_____

_____

DATE: _____ **PLACE:** _____ **BUDGET:** _____

---✦---

3 things I did today:

01. _____

02. _____

03. _____

Favorite thing I ate today:

_____

One person I met today (name, age, where they are from):

_____

One thing I learned about the world today:

_____

One thing I learned about myself today:

_____

One thing I will do different tomorrow:

_____

General thoughts about today:

_____

_____

_____

DATE: _____   PLACE: _____   BUDGET: _____

"The value of your travels does not hinge on how many stamps you have in your passport when you get home." — Rolf Potts

3 things I did today:

01. _____

02. _____

03. _____

Favorite thing I ate today:

_____

One person I met today (name, age, where they are from):

_____

One thing I learned about the world today:

_____

One thing I learned about myself today:

_____

One thing I will do different tomorrow:

_____

General thoughts about today:

_____

_____

_____

DATE: _____ **PLACE:** _____ **BUDGET:** _____

3 things I did today:

01. _____

02. _____

03. _____

Favorite thing I ate today:

_____

One person I met today (name, age, where they are from):

_____

One thing I learned about the world today:

_____

One thing I learned about myself today:

_____

One thing I will do different tomorrow:

_____

General thoughts about today:

_____

_____

_____

DATE: _____   PLACE: _____   BUDGET: _____

"There are no shortcuts to any place worth going."
— Beverly Sills

3 things I did today:

01. _____

02. _____

03. _____

Favorite thing I ate today:

_____

One person I met today (name, age, where they are from):

_____

One thing I learned about the world today:

_____

One thing I learned about myself today:

_____

One thing I will do different tomorrow:

_____

General thoughts about today:

_____

_____

_____

DATE: _____   **PLACE:** _____   **BUDGET:** _____

--------------◆--------------

3 things I did today:

01. _____

02. _____

03. _____

Favorite thing I ate today:

_____

One person I met today (name, age, where they are from):

_____

One thing I learned about the world today:

_____

One thing I learned about myself today:

_____

One thing I will do different tomorrow:

_____

General thoughts about today:

_____

_____

_____

DATE: _____ **PLACE:** _____ **BUDGET:** _____

"A person susceptible to 'wanderlust' is not so much addicted to movement as committed to transformation." — Pico Iyer

3 things I did today:

01. _____

02. _____

03. _____

Favorite thing I ate today:

_____

One person I met today (name, age, where they are from):

_____

One thing I learned about the world today:

_____

One thing I learned about myself today:

_____

One thing I will do different tomorrow:

_____

General thoughts about today:

_____

_____

_____

DATE: _____ **PLACE:** _____ **BUDGET:** _____

---◆---

3 things I did today:

01. _____

02. _____

03. _____

Favorite thing I ate today:

_____

One person I met today (name, age, where they are from):

_____

One thing I learned about the world today:

_____

One thing I learned about myself today:

_____

One thing I will do different tomorrow:

_____

General thoughts about today:

_____

_____

_____

DATE: _____ **PLACE:** _____ **BUDGET:** _____

"When preparing to travel, lay out all your clothes and all your money. Then take half the clothes and twice the money." — Susan Heller

3 things I did today:

01. _____

02. _____

03. _____

Favorite thing I ate today:

_____

One person I met today (name, age, where they are from):

_____

One thing I learned about the world today:

_____

One thing I learned about myself today:

_____

One thing I will do different tomorrow:

_____

General thoughts about today:

_____

_____

_____

DATE: _____ **PLACE:** _____ **BUDGET:** _____

———————————— ✦ ————————————

3 things I did today:

01. _____

02. _____

03. _____

Favorite thing I ate today:

_____

One person I met today (name, age, where they are from):

_____

One thing I learned about the world today:

_____

One thing I learned about myself today:

_____

One thing I will do different tomorrow:

_____

General thoughts about today:

_____

_____

_____

DATE: _____ PLACE: _____ BUDGET: _____

"Experience, travel – these are as education in themselves."
— Euripides

3 things I did today:

01. _____

02. _____

03. _____

Favorite thing I ate today:

_____

One person I met today (name, age, where they are from):

_____

One thing I learned about the world today:

_____

One thing I learned about myself today:

_____

One thing I will do different tomorrow:

_____

General thoughts about today:

_____

_____

_____

DATE: _____   **PLACE:** _____   **BUDGET:** _____

———————————◆———————————

3 things I did today:

01. _____

02. _____

03. _____

Favorite thing I ate today:

_____

One person I met today (name, age, where they are from):

_____

One thing I learned about the world today:

_____

One thing I learned about myself today:

_____

One thing I will do different tomorrow:

_____

General thoughts about today:

_____

_____

_____

DATE: _____   **PLACE:** _____   **BUDGET:** _____

"Travel is never a matter of money but of courage."
— Paolo Coelho

3 things I did today:

01. _____

02. _____

03. _____

Favorite thing I ate today:

_____

One person I met today (name, age, where they are from):

_____

One thing I learned about the world today:

_____

One thing I learned about myself today:

_____

One thing I will do different tomorrow:

_____

General thoughts about today:

_____

_____

_____

DATE: _____ **PLACE:** _____ **BUDGET:** _____

————————◆————————

3 things I did today:

01. _____

02. _____

03. _____

Favorite thing I ate today:

_____

One person I met today (name, age, where they are from):

_____

One thing I learned about the world today:

_____

One thing I learned about myself today:

_____

One thing I will do different tomorrow:

_____

General thoughts about today:

_____

_____

_____

DATE: _____   PLACE: _____   BUDGET: _____

"There are no foreign lands. It is the traveler only who is foreign."
— Robert Louis Stevenson

3 things I did today:

01. _____

02. _____

03. _____

Favorite thing I ate today:

_____

One person I met today (name, age, where they are from):

_____

One thing I learned about the world today:

_____

One thing I learned about myself today:

_____

One thing I will do different tomorrow:

_____

General thoughts about today:

_____

_____

_____

DATE: _____ **PLACE:** _____ **BUDGET:** _____

———————————————— ✦ ————————————————

3 things I did today:

01. _____

02. _____

03. _____

Favorite thing I ate today:

_____

One person I met today (name, age, where they are from):

_____

One thing I learned about the world today:

_____

One thing I learned about myself today:

_____

One thing I will do different tomorrow:

_____

General thoughts about today:

_____

_____

_____

DATE: _____ **PLACE:** _____ **BUDGET:** _____

"Part of the urge to explore is a desire to become lost."
— Tracy Johnston

3 things I did today:

01. _____

02. _____

03. _____

Favorite thing I ate today:

_____

One person I met today (name, age, where they are from):

_____

One thing I learned about the world today:

_____

One thing I learned about myself today:

_____

One thing I will do different tomorrow:

_____

General thoughts about today:

_____

_____

_____

DATE: _____ **PLACE:** _____ **BUDGET:** _____

———————————◈———————————

3 things I did today:

01. _____

02. _____

03. _____

Favorite thing I ate today:

_____

One person I met today (name, age, where they are from):

_____

One thing I learned about the world today:

_____

One thing I learned about myself today:

_____

One thing I will do different tomorrow:

_____

General thoughts about today:

_____

_____

_____

DATE: _____ **PLACE:** _____ **BUDGET:** _____

"Nothing lasts forever, except the day before you start your vacation."
— Gayland Anderson

3 things I did today:

01. _____

02. _____

03. _____

Favorite thing I ate today:

_____

One person I met today (name, age, where they are from):

_____

One thing I learned about the world today:

_____

One thing I learned about myself today:

_____

One thing I will do different tomorrow:

_____

General thoughts about today:

_____

_____

_____

DATE: _____   **PLACE:** _____   **BUDGET:** _____

———————————— ✦ ————————————

3 things I did today:

01. _____

02. _____

03. _____

Favorite thing I ate today:

_____

One person I met today (name, age, where they are from):

_____

One thing I learned about the world today:

_____

One thing I learned about myself today:

_____

One thing I will do different tomorrow:

_____

General thoughts about today:

_____

_____

_____

"Don't be afraid to give up the good to go for the great."
— John D. Rockefeller

3 things I did today:

01. _____

02. _____

03. _____

Favorite thing I ate today:

_____

One person I met today (name, age, where they are from):

_____

One thing I learned about the world today:

_____

One thing I learned about myself today:

_____

One thing I will do different tomorrow:

_____

General thoughts about today:

_____

_____

_____

DATE: _____ **PLACE:** _____ **BUDGET:** _____

———————————◆———————————

3 things I did today:

01. _____

02. _____

03. _____

Favorite thing I ate today:

_____

One person I met today (name, age, where they are from):

_____

One thing I learned about the world today:

_____

One thing I learned about myself today:

_____

One thing I will do different tomorrow:

_____

General thoughts about today:

_____

_____

_____

DATE: _____   **PLACE:** _____   **BUDGET:** _____

"Paris is always a good idea."
— Audrey Hepburn

3 things I did today:

01. _____

02. _____

03. _____

Favorite thing I ate today:

_____

One person I met today (name, age, where they are from):

_____

One thing I learned about the world today:

_____

One thing I learned about myself today:

_____

One thing I will do different tomorrow:

_____

General thoughts about today:

_____

_____

_____

DATE: _____   **PLACE:** _____   **BUDGET:** _____

---✦---

3 things I did today:

01. _____

02. _____

03. _____

Favorite thing I ate today:

_____

One person I met today (name, age, where they are from):

_____

One thing I learned about the world today:

_____

One thing I learned about myself today:

_____

One thing I will do different tomorrow:

_____

General thoughts about today:

_____

_____

_____

DATE: _____   **PLACE:** _____   **BUDGET:** _____

"Wandering re-establishes the original harmony which once existed between man and the universe." — Anatole France

3 things I did today:

01. _____

02. _____

03. _____

Favorite thing I ate today:

_____

One person I met today (name, age, where they are from):

_____

One thing I learned about the world today:

_____

One thing I learned about myself today:

_____

One thing I will do different tomorrow:

_____

General thoughts about today:

_____

_____

_____

DATE: _____   **PLACE:** _____   **BUDGET:** _____

---◆---

3 things I did today:

01. _____

02. _____

03. _____

Favorite thing I ate today:

_____

One person I met today (name, age, where they are from):

_____

One thing I learned about the world today:

_____

One thing I learned about myself today:

_____

One thing I will do different tomorrow:

_____

General thoughts about today:

_____

_____

_____

DATE: _____ **PLACE:** _____ **BUDGET:** _____

"I haven't been everywhere, but it's on my list."
— Susan Sontag

3 things I did today:

01. _____

02. _____

03. _____

Favorite thing I ate today:

_____

One person I met today (name, age, where they are from):

_____

One thing I learned about the world today:

_____

One thing I learned about myself today:

_____

One thing I will do different tomorrow:

_____

General thoughts about today:

_____

_____

_____

———————————————— ✦ ————————————————

3 things I did today:

01. _____

02. _____

03. _____

Favorite thing I ate today:

_____

One person I met today (name, age, where they are from):

_____

One thing I learned about the world today:

_____

One thing I learned about myself today:

_____

One thing I will do different tomorrow:

_____

General thoughts about today:

_____

_____

_____

DATE: _____   **PLACE:** _____   **BUDGET:** _____

"Travel makes one modest, you see what a tiny place you occupy in the world."
— Gustave Flaubert

3 things I did today:

01. _____

02. _____

03. _____

Favorite thing I ate today:

_____

One person I met today (name, age, where they are from):

_____

One thing I learned about the world today:

_____

One thing I learned about myself today:

_____

One thing I will do different tomorrow:

_____

General thoughts about today:

_____

_____

_____

DATE: _____   **PLACE:** _____   **BUDGET:** _____

———————————— ✦ ————————————

3 things I did today:

01. _____

02. _____

03. _____

Favorite thing I ate today:

_____

One person I met today (name, age, where they are from):

_____

One thing I learned about the world today:

_____

One thing I learned about myself today:

_____

One thing I will do different tomorrow:

_____

General thoughts about today:

_____

_____

_____

DATE: _____   **PLACE:** _____   **BUDGET:** _____

"Traveling's not something you're good at. It's something you do. Like breathing."
— Gayle Foreman

3 things I did today:

01. _____

02. _____

03. _____

Favorite thing I ate today:

_____

One person I met today (name, age, where they are from):

_____

One thing I learned about the world today:

_____

One thing I learned about myself today:

_____

One thing I will do different tomorrow:

_____

General thoughts about today:

_____

_____

_____

DATE: _____   **PLACE:** _____   **BUDGET:** _____

———————————— ✦ ————————————

3 things I did today:

01. _____

02. _____

03. _____

Favorite thing I ate today:

_____

One person I met today (name, age, where they are from):

_____

One thing I learned about the world today:

_____

One thing I learned about myself today:

_____

One thing I will do different tomorrow:

_____

General thoughts about today:

_____

_____

_____

"The privilege of a lifetime is to become who you truly are."
— Carl Jung

3 things I did today:

01. _____

02. _____

03. _____

Favorite thing I ate today:

_____

One person I met today (name, age, where they are from):

_____

One thing I learned about the world today:

_____

One thing I learned about myself today:

_____

One thing I will do different tomorrow:

_____

General thoughts about today:

_____

_____

_____

DATE: _____   **PLACE:** _____   **BUDGET:** _____

---

3 things I did today:

01. _____

02. _____

03. _____

Favorite thing I ate today:

_____

One person I met today (name, age, where they are from):

_____

One thing I learned about the world today:

_____

One thing I learned about myself today:

_____

One thing I will do different tomorrow:

_____

General thoughts about today:

_____

_____

_____

DATE: _____   **PLACE:** _____   **BUDGET:** _____

"Tourists don't know where they've been, travelers don't know where they're going." — Paul Theroux

3 things I did today:

01. _____

02. _____

03. _____

Favorite thing I ate today:

_____

One person I met today (name, age, where they are from):

_____

One thing I learned about the world today:

_____

One thing I learned about myself today:

_____

One thing I will do different tomorrow:

_____

General thoughts about today:

_____

_____

_____

DATE: _____   **PLACE:** _____   **BUDGET:** _____

———————— ✦ ————————

3 things I did today:

01. _____

02. _____

03. _____

Favorite thing I ate today:

_____

One person I met today (name, age, where they are from):

_____

One thing I learned about the world today:

_____

One thing I learned about myself today:

_____

One thing I will do different tomorrow:

_____

General thoughts about today:

_____

_____

_____

DATE: _____ **PLACE:** _____ **BUDGET:** _____

"The biggest adventure you can take is to live the life of your dreams."
— Oprah Winfrey

3 things I did today:

01. _____

02. _____

03. _____

Favorite thing I ate today:

_____

One person I met today (name, age, where they are from):

_____

One thing I learned about the world today:

_____

One thing I learned about myself today:

_____

One thing I will do different tomorrow:

_____

General thoughts about today:

_____

_____

_____

DATE: _____ **PLACE:** _____ **BUDGET:** _____

---◆---

3 things I did today:

01. _____

02. _____

03. _____

Favorite thing I ate today:

_____

One person I met today (name, age, where they are from):

_____

One thing I learned about the world today:

_____

One thing I learned about myself today:

_____

One thing I will do different tomorrow:

_____

General thoughts about today:

_____

_____

_____

DATE: _____   **PLACE:** _____   **BUDGET:** _____

"For my part, I travel not to go anywhere, but to go. I travel for travel's sake.
The great affair is to move." — Robert Louis Stevenson

3 things I did today:

01. _____

02. _____

03. _____

Favorite thing I ate today:

_____

One person I met today (name, age, where they are from):

_____

One thing I learned about the world today:

_____

One thing I learned about myself today:

_____

One thing I will do different tomorrow:

_____

General thoughts about today:

_____

_____

_____

DATE: _____   **PLACE:** _____   **BUDGET:** _____

---

3 things I did today:

01. _____

02. _____

03. _____

Favorite thing I ate today:

_____

One person I met today (name, age, where they are from):

_____

One thing I learned about the world today:

_____

One thing I learned about myself today:

_____

One thing I will do different tomorrow:

_____

General thoughts about today:

_____

_____

_____

"I'm not afraid of storms, for I'm learning how to sail my ship."
— Louisa May Alcott

3 things I did today:

01. _____

02. _____

03. _____

Favorite thing I ate today:

_____

One person I met today (name, age, where they are from):

_____

One thing I learned about the world today:

_____

One thing I learned about myself today:

_____

One thing I will do different tomorrow:

_____

General thoughts about today:

_____

_____

_____

DATE: _____   **PLACE:** _____   **BUDGET:** _____

—————————◆—————————

3 things I did today:

01. _____

02. _____

03. _____

Favorite thing I ate today:

_____

One person I met today (name, age, where they are from):

_____

One thing I learned about the world today:

_____

One thing I learned about myself today:

_____

One thing I will do different tomorrow:

_____

General thoughts about today:

_____

_____

_____

DATE: _____   **PLACE:** _____   **BUDGET:** _____

"You need not even listen, just wait...the world will offer itself freely to you, unmasking itself." — Franz Kafka

3 things I did today:

01. _____

02. _____

03. _____

Favorite thing I ate today:

_____

One person I met today (name, age, where they are from):

_____

One thing I learned about the world today:

_____

One thing I learned about myself today:

_____

One thing I will do different tomorrow:

_____

General thoughts about today:

_____

_____

_____

DATE: _____   **PLACE:** _____   **BUDGET:** _____

---◆---

3 things I did today:

01. _____

02. _____

03. _____

Favorite thing I ate today:

_____

One person I met today (name, age, where they are from):

_____

One thing I learned about the world today:

_____

One thing I learned about myself today:

_____

One thing I will do different tomorrow:

_____

General thoughts about today:

_____

_____

_____

"Hardship often prepares an ordinary person for an extraordinary destiny."
— Christopher Markus

3 things I did today:

01. _____

02. _____

03. _____

Favorite thing I ate today:

_____

One person I met today (name, age, where they are from):

_____

One thing I learned about the world today:

_____

One thing I learned about myself today:

_____

One thing I will do different tomorrow:

_____

General thoughts about today:

_____

_____

_____

DATE: _____ **PLACE:** _____ **BUDGET:** _____

---◆---

3 things I did today:

01. _____

02. _____

03. _____

Favorite thing I ate today:

_____

One person I met today (name, age, where they are from):

_____

One thing I learned about the world today:

_____

One thing I learned about myself today:

_____

One thing I will do different tomorrow:

_____

General thoughts about today:

_____

_____

_____

DATE: _____ **PLACE:** _____ **BUDGET:** _____

"A journey is best measured in friends, rather than miles."
— Tim Cahill

3 things I did today:

01. _____

02. _____

03. _____

Favorite thing I ate today:

_____

One person I met today (name, age, where they are from):

_____

One thing I learned about the world today:

_____

One thing I learned about myself today:

_____

One thing I will do different tomorrow:

_____

General thoughts about today:

_____

_____

_____

DATE: _____   **PLACE:** _____   **BUDGET:** _____

———————— ✦ ————————

3 things I did today:

01. _____

02. _____

03. _____

Favorite thing I ate today:

_____

One person I met today (name, age, where they are from):

_____

One thing I learned about the world today:

_____

One thing I learned about myself today:

_____

One thing I will do different tomorrow:

_____

General thoughts about today:

_____

_____

_____

DATE: _____   **PLACE:** _____   **BUDGET:** _____

"Start where you are. Use what you have. Do what you can."
— Arthur Ashe

3 things I did today:

01. _____

02. _____

03. _____

Favorite thing I ate today:

_____

One person I met today (name, age, where they are from):

_____

One thing I learned about the world today:

_____

One thing I learned about myself today:

_____

One thing I will do different tomorrow:

_____

General thoughts about today:

_____

_____

_____

DATE: _____   **PLACE:** _____   **BUDGET:** _____

———————————✦———————————

3 things I did today:

01. _____

02. _____

03. _____

Favorite thing I ate today:

_____

One person I met today (name, age, where they are from):

_____

One thing I learned about the world today:

_____

One thing I learned about myself today:

_____

One thing I will do different tomorrow:

_____

General thoughts about today:

_____

_____

_____

"Where you come from does matter — but not nearly as much as where you are headed." — Jodi Picoult

3 things I did today:

01. _____

02. _____

03. _____

Favorite thing I ate today:

_____

One person I met today (name, age, where they are from):

_____

One thing I learned about the world today:

_____

One thing I learned about myself today:

_____

One thing I will do different tomorrow:

_____

General thoughts about today:

_____

_____

_____

DATE: _____   **PLACE:** _____   **BUDGET:** _____

———————————— ✦ ————————————

3 things I did today:

01. _____

02. _____

03. _____

Favorite thing I ate today:

_____

One person I met today (name, age, where they are from):

_____

One thing I learned about the world today:

_____

One thing I learned about myself today:

_____

One thing I will do different tomorrow:

_____

General thoughts about today:

_____

_____

_____

DATE: _____   **PLACE:** _____   **BUDGET:** _____

> "It is never too late to be what you might have been."
> — George Eliot

3 things I did today:

01. _____

02. _____

03. _____

Favorite thing I ate today:

_____

One person I met today (name, age, where they are from):

_____

One thing I learned about the world today:

_____

One thing I learned about myself today:

_____

One thing I will do different tomorrow:

_____

General thoughts about today:

_____

_____

_____

DATE: _____ **PLACE:** _____ **BUDGET:** _____

---

3 things I did today:

01. _____

02. _____

03. _____

Favorite thing I ate today:

_____

One person I met today (name, age, where they are from):

_____

One thing I learned about the world today:

_____

One thing I learned about myself today:

_____

One thing I will do different tomorrow:

_____

General thoughts about today:

_____

_____

_____

DATE: _____ **PLACE:** _____ **BUDGET:** _____

"All journeys have secret destinations of which the traveler is unaware."
— Marin Buber

3 things I did today:

01. _____

02. _____

03. _____

Favorite thing I ate today:

_____

One person I met today (name, age, where they are from):

_____

One thing I learned about the world today:

_____

One thing I learned about myself today:

_____

One thing I will do different tomorrow:

_____

General thoughts about today:

_____

_____

_____

DATE: _____ **PLACE:** _____ **BUDGET:** _____

———————————— ✦ ————————————

3 things I did today:

01. _____

02. _____

03. _____

Favorite thing I ate today:

_____

One person I met today (name, age, where they are from):

_____

One thing I learned about the world today:

_____

One thing I learned about myself today:

_____

One thing I will do different tomorrow:

_____

General thoughts about today:

_____

_____

_____

DATE: _____   PLACE: _____   BUDGET: _____

"Adventure should be part of everyone's life. It is the whole difference between being fully alive and just existing." — Holly Morris

3 things I did today:

01. _____

02. _____

03. _____

Favorite thing I ate today:

_____

One person I met today (name, age, where they are from):

_____

One thing I learned about the world today:

_____

One thing I learned about myself today:

_____

One thing I will do different tomorrow:

_____

General thoughts about today:

_____

_____

_____

DATE: _____ **PLACE:** _____ **BUDGET:** _____

---❖---

3 things I did today:

01. _____

02. _____

03. _____

Favorite thing I ate today:

_____

One person I met today (name, age, where they are from):

_____

One thing I learned about the world today:

_____

One thing I learned about myself today:

_____

One thing I will do different tomorrow:

_____

General thoughts about today:

_____

_____

_____

DATE: _____   **PLACE:** _____   **BUDGET:** _____

"So much better to travel than to arrive."
— Margaret Atwood

3 things I did today:

01. _____

02. _____

03. _____

Favorite thing I ate today:

_____

One person I met today (name, age, where they are from):

_____

One thing I learned about the world today:

_____

One thing I learned about myself today:

_____

One thing I will do different tomorrow:

_____

General thoughts about today:

_____

_____

_____

DATE: _____ PLACE: _____ BUDGET: _____

———————————— ✦ ————————————

3 things I did today:

01. _____

02. _____

03. _____

Favorite thing I ate today:

_____

One person I met today (name, age, where they are from):

_____

One thing I learned about the world today:

_____

One thing I learned about myself today:

_____

One thing I will do different tomorrow:

_____

General thoughts about today:

_____

_____

_____

DATE: _____   PLACE: _____   BUDGET: _____

"A wise traveler never despises his own country."
— Carlo Goldini

3 things I did today:

01. _____

02. _____

03. _____

Favorite thing I ate today:

_____

One person I met today (name, age, where they are from):

_____

One thing I learned about the world today:

_____

One thing I learned about myself today:

_____

One thing I will do different tomorrow:

_____

General thoughts about today:

_____

_____

_____

DATE: _____ **PLACE:** _____ **BUDGET:** _____

———————————◆———————————

3 things I did today:

01. _____

02. _____

03. _____

Favorite thing I ate today:

_____

One person I met today (name, age, where they are from):

_____

One thing I learned about the world today:

_____

One thing I learned about myself today:

_____

One thing I will do different tomorrow:

_____

General thoughts about today:

_____

_____

_____

DATE: _____   PLACE: _____   BUDGET: _____

"We do not describe the world we see. We see the world we can describe."
— René Descartes

3 things I did today:

01. _____

02. _____

03. _____

Favorite thing I ate today:

_____

One person I met today (name, age, where they are from):

_____

One thing I learned about the world today:

_____

One thing I learned about myself today:

_____

One thing I will do different tomorrow:

_____

General thoughts about today:

_____

_____

_____

———————————— ✦ ————————————

3 things I did today:

01. _____

02. _____

03. _____

Favorite thing I ate today:

_____

One person I met today (name, age, where they are from):

_____

One thing I learned about the world today:

_____

One thing I learned about myself today:

_____

One thing I will do different tomorrow:

_____

General thoughts about today:

_____

_____

_____

DATE: _____ **PLACE:** _____ **BUDGET:** _____

"You only live once, but if you do it right, once is enough."
— Mae West

3 things I did today:

01. _____

02. _____

03. _____

Favorite thing I ate today:

_____

One person I met today (name, age, where they are from):

_____

One thing I learned about the world today:

_____

One thing I learned about myself today:

_____

One thing I will do different tomorrow:

_____

General thoughts about today:

_____

_____

_____

DATE: _____   **PLACE:** _____   **BUDGET:** _____

───────────── ✦ ─────────────

3 things I did today:

01. _____

02. _____

03. _____

Favorite thing I ate today:

_____

One person I met today (name, age, where they are from):

_____

One thing I learned about the world today:

_____

One thing I learned about myself today:

_____

One thing I will do different tomorrow:

_____

General thoughts about today:

_____

_____

_____

DATE: _____   PLACE: _____   BUDGET: _____

"Don't live your life through what-ifs, live it with I knows."
— Marco Zuniga

3 things I did today:

01. _____

02. _____

03. _____

Favorite thing I ate today:

_____

One person I met today (name, age, where they are from):

_____

One thing I learned about the world today:

_____

One thing I learned about myself today:

_____

One thing I will do different tomorrow:

_____

General thoughts about today:

_____

_____

_____

DATE: _____   **PLACE:** _____   **BUDGET:** _____

————————————— ✦ —————————————

3 things I did today:

01. _____

02. _____

03. _____

Favorite thing I ate today:

_____

One person I met today (name, age, where they are from):

_____

One thing I learned about the world today:

_____

One thing I learned about myself today:

_____

One thing I will do different tomorrow:

_____

General thoughts about today:

_____

_____

_____

DATE: _____   **PLACE:** _____   **BUDGET:** _____

"The impulse to travel is one of the hopeful symptoms of life."
— Agnes Repplier

3 things I did today:

01. _____

02. _____

03. _____

Favorite thing I ate today:

_____

One person I met today (name, age, where they are from):

_____

One thing I learned about the world today:

_____

One thing I learned about myself today:

_____

One thing I will do different tomorrow:

_____

General thoughts about today:

_____

_____

_____

DATE: _____ **PLACE:** _____ **BUDGET:** _____

───────────────◆───────────────

3 things I did today:

01. _____

02. _____

03. _____

Favorite thing I ate today:

_____

One person I met today (name, age, where they are from):

_____

One thing I learned about the world today:

_____

One thing I learned about myself today:

_____

One thing I will do different tomorrow:

_____

General thoughts about today:

_____

_____

_____

DATE: _____   **PLACE:** _____   **BUDGET:** _____

"A year from now, you will wish you had started today."

— Karen Lamb

3 things I did today:

01. _____

02. _____

03. _____

Favorite thing I ate today:

_____

One person I met today (name, age, where they are from):

_____

One thing I learned about the world today:

_____

One thing I learned about myself today:

_____

One thing I will do different tomorrow:

_____

General thoughts about today:

_____

_____

_____

———————— ✦ ————————

3 things I did today:

01. _____

02. _____

03. _____

Favorite thing I ate today:

_____

One person I met today (name, age, where they are from):

_____

One thing I learned about the world today:

_____

One thing I learned about myself today:

_____

One thing I will do different tomorrow:

_____

General thoughts about today:

_____

_____

_____

"I don't know where I am going, but I'm on my way."
— Carl Sagan

3 things I did today:

01. _____

02. _____

03. _____

Favorite thing I ate today:

_____

One person I met today (name, age, where they are from):

_____

One thing I learned about the world today:

_____

One thing I learned about myself today:

_____

One thing I will do different tomorrow:

_____

General thoughts about today:

_____

_____

_____

DATE: _____ **PLACE:** _____ **BUDGET:** _____

———————— ✦ ————————

3 things I did today:

01. _____

02. _____

03. _____

Favorite thing I ate today:

_____

One person I met today (name, age, where they are from):

_____

One thing I learned about the world today:

_____

One thing I learned about myself today:

_____

One thing I will do different tomorrow:

_____

General thoughts about today:

_____

_____

_____

DATE: _____   PLACE: _____   BUDGET: _____

"When you travel, remember that a foreign country is not designed to make you comfortable. It is designed to make its own people comfortable." — Clifton Fadiman

3 things I did today:

01. _____

02. _____

03. _____

Favorite thing I ate today:

_____

One person I met today (name, age, where they are from):

_____

One thing I learned about the world today:

_____

One thing I learned about myself today:

_____

One thing I will do different tomorrow:

_____

General thoughts about today:

_____

_____

_____

DATE: _____   **PLACE:** _____   **BUDGET:** _____

—————————— ✦ ——————————

3 things I did today:

01. _____

02. _____

03. _____

Favorite thing I ate today:

_____

One person I met today (name, age, where they are from):

_____

One thing I learned about the world today:

_____

One thing I learned about myself today:

_____

One thing I will do different tomorrow:

_____

General thoughts about today:

_____

_____

_____

DATE: _____ **PLACE:** _____ **BUDGET:** _____

"In three words I can sum up everything I've learned about life: it goes on."
— Robert Frost

3 things I did today:

01. _____

02. _____

03. _____

Favorite thing I ate today:

_____

One person I met today (name, age, where they are from):

_____

One thing I learned about the world today:

_____

One thing I learned about myself today:

_____

One thing I will do different tomorrow:

_____

General thoughts about today:

_____

_____

_____

DATE: _____ **PLACE:** _____ **BUDGET:** _____

—————————— ✦ ——————————

3 things I did today:

01. _____

02. _____

03. _____

Favorite thing I ate today:

_____

One person I met today (name, age, where they are from):

_____

One thing I learned about the world today:

_____

One thing I learned about myself today:

_____

One thing I will do different tomorrow:

_____

General thoughts about today:

_____

_____

_____

DATE: _____   **PLACE:** _____   **BUDGET:** _____

"Travel expands the mind and fills the gap."
— Sheda Savage

3 things I did today:

01. _____

02. _____

03. _____

Favorite thing I ate today:

_____

One person I met today (name, age, where they are from):

_____

One thing I learned about the world today:

_____

One thing I learned about myself today:

_____

One thing I will do different tomorrow:

_____

General thoughts about today:

_____

_____

_____

DATE: _____ **PLACE:** _____ **BUDGET:** _____

———————————— ✦ ————————————

3 things I did today:

01. _____

02. _____

03. _____

Favorite thing I ate today:

_____

One person I met today (name, age, where they are from):

_____

One thing I learned about the world today:

_____

One thing I learned about myself today:

_____

One thing I will do different tomorrow:

_____

General thoughts about today:

_____

_____

_____

DATE: _____   **PLACE:** _____   **BUDGET:** _____

"The mind is furnished with ideas by experience alone."
— John Locke

3 things I did today:

01. _____

02. _____

03. _____

Favorite thing I ate today:

_____

One person I met today (name, age, where they are from):

_____

One thing I learned about the world today:

_____

One thing I learned about myself today:

_____

One thing I will do different tomorrow:

_____

General thoughts about today:

_____

_____

_____

DATE: _____ **PLACE:** _____ **BUDGET:** _____

---✦---

3 things I did today:

01. _____

02. _____

03. _____

Favorite thing I ate today:

_____

One person I met today (name, age, where they are from):

_____

One thing I learned about the world today:

_____

One thing I learned about myself today:

_____

One thing I will do different tomorrow:

_____

General thoughts about today:

_____

_____

_____

DATE: _____ **PLACE:** _____ **BUDGET:** _____

"It is good to have an end to journey toward; but it is the journey that matters, in the end." — Ernest Hemingway

3 things I did today:

01. _____

02. _____

03. _____

Favorite thing I ate today:

_____

One person I met today (name, age, where they are from):

_____

One thing I learned about the world today:

_____

One thing I learned about myself today:

_____

One thing I will do different tomorrow:

_____

General thoughts about today:

_____

_____

_____

DATE: _____   **PLACE:** _____   **BUDGET:** _____

———————————— ✦ ————————————

3 things I did today:

01. _____

02. _____

03. _____

Favorite thing I ate today:

_____

One person I met today (name, age, where they are from):

_____

One thing I learned about the world today:

_____

One thing I learned about myself today:

_____

One thing I will do different tomorrow:

_____

General thoughts about today:

_____

_____

_____

DATE: _____   **PLACE:** _____   **BUDGET:** _____

"Two roads diverged in a wood and I – I took the one less traveled by."
— Robert Frost

3 things I did today:

01. _____

02. _____

03. _____

Favorite thing I ate today:

_____

One person I met today (name, age, where they are from):

_____

One thing I learned about the world today:

_____

One thing I learned about myself today:

_____

One thing I will do different tomorrow:

_____

General thoughts about today:

_____

_____

_____

DATE: _____ **PLACE:** _____ **BUDGET:** _____

————————————————✦————————————————

3 things I did today:

01. _____

02. _____

03. _____

Favorite thing I ate today:

_____

One person I met today (name, age, where they are from):

_____

One thing I learned about the world today:

_____

One thing I learned about myself today:

_____

One thing I will do different tomorrow:

_____

General thoughts about today:

_____

_____

_____

DATE: _____   **PLACE:** _____   **BUDGET:** _____

"If you wish to travel far and fast, travel light. Take off all your envies, jealousies, unforgiveness, selfishness and fears." — Cesare Pavese

3 things I did today:

01. _____

02. _____

03. _____

Favorite thing I ate today:

_____

One person I met today (name, age, where they are from):

_____

One thing I learned about the world today:

_____

One thing I learned about myself today:

_____

One thing I will do different tomorrow:

_____

General thoughts about today:

_____

_____

_____

DATE: _____   **PLACE:** _____   **BUDGET:** _____

---

3 things I did today:

01. _____

02. _____

03. _____

Favorite thing I ate today:

_____

One person I met today (name, age, where they are from):

_____

One thing I learned about the world today:

_____

One thing I learned about myself today:

_____

One thing I will do different tomorrow:

_____

General thoughts about today:

_____

_____

_____

DATE: _____   **PLACE:** _____   **BUDGET:** _____

"A ship in a harbor is safe, but it is not what ships are built for."
— John A. Shedd

3 things I did today:

01. _____

02. _____

03. _____

Favorite thing I ate today:

_____

One person I met today (name, age, where they are from):

_____

One thing I learned about the world today:

_____

One thing I learned about myself today:

_____

One thing I will do different tomorrow:

_____

General thoughts about today:

_____

_____

_____

DATE: _____   **PLACE:** _____   **BUDGET:** _____

---◆---

3 things I did today:

01. _____

02. _____

03. _____

Favorite thing I ate today:

_____

One person I met today (name, age, where they are from):

_____

One thing I learned about the world today:

_____

One thing I learned about myself today:

_____

One thing I will do different tomorrow:

_____

General thoughts about today:

_____

_____

_____

DATE: _____   **PLACE:** _____   **BUDGET:** _____

"Once the travel bug bites, there is no known antidote and I know that I shall be happily infected until the end of my life." — Michael Palin

3 things I did today:

01. _____

02. _____

03. _____

Favorite thing I ate today:

_____

One person I met today (name, age, where they are from):

_____

One thing I learned about the world today:

_____

One thing I learned about myself today:

_____

One thing I will do different tomorrow:

_____

General thoughts about today:

_____

_____

_____

DATE: _____   **PLACE:** _____   **BUDGET:** _____

———————◆———————

3 things I did today:

01. _____

02. _____

03. _____

Favorite thing I ate today:

_____

One person I met today (name, age, where they are from):

_____

One thing I learned about the world today:

_____

One thing I learned about myself today:

_____

One thing I will do different tomorrow:

_____

General thoughts about today:

_____

_____

_____

DATE: _____ **PLACE:** _____ **BUDGET:** _____

"Do not dare not to dare."
— C.S. Lewis

3 things I did today:

01. _____

02. _____

03. _____

Favorite thing I ate today:

_____

One person I met today (name, age, where they are from):

_____

One thing I learned about the world today:

_____

One thing I learned about myself today:

_____

One thing I will do different tomorrow:

_____

General thoughts about today:

_____

_____

_____

DATE: _____   PLACE: _____   BUDGET: _____

———————————◆———————————

3 things I did today:

01. _____

02. _____

03. _____

Favorite thing I ate today:

_____

One person I met today (name, age, where they are from):

_____

One thing I learned about the world today:

_____

One thing I learned about myself today:

_____

One thing I will do different tomorrow:

_____

General thoughts about today:

_____

_____

_____

DATE: _____ **PLACE:** _____ **BUDGET:** _____

"Thinking. The talking of the soul with itself."
— Plato

3 things I did today:

01. _____

02. _____

03. _____

Favorite thing I ate today:

_____

One person I met today (name, age, where they are from):

_____

One thing I learned about the world today:

_____

One thing I learned about myself today:

_____

One thing I will do different tomorrow:

_____

General thoughts about today:

_____

_____

_____

DATE: _____ **PLACE:** _____ **BUDGET:** _____

---

3 things I did today:

01. _____

02. _____

03. _____

Favorite thing I ate today:

_____

One person I met today (name, age, where they are from):

_____

One thing I learned about the world today:

_____

One thing I learned about myself today:

_____

One thing I will do different tomorrow:

_____

General thoughts about today:

_____

_____

_____

"When all's said and done, all roads lead to the same end. So it's not so much which road you take, as how you take it." — Charles de Lint

3 things I did today:

01. _____

02. _____

03. _____

Favorite thing I ate today:

_____

One person I met today (name, age, where they are from):

_____

One thing I learned about the world today:

_____

One thing I learned about myself today:

_____

One thing I will do different tomorrow:

_____

General thoughts about today:

_____

_____

_____

DATE: _____   **PLACE:** _____   **BUDGET:** _____

———————◈———————

3 things I did today:

01. _____

02. _____

03. _____

Favorite thing I ate today:

_____

One person I met today (name, age, where they are from):

_____

One thing I learned about the world today:

_____

One thing I learned about myself today:

_____

One thing I will do different tomorrow:

_____

General thoughts about today:

_____

_____

_____

DATE: _____   PLACE: _____   BUDGET: _____

"People travel to faraway places to watch, in fascination, the people they
ignore at home." — Dagobert D. Runes

3 things I did today:

01. _____

02. _____

03. _____

Favorite thing I ate today:

_____

One person I met today (name, age, where they are from):

_____

One thing I learned about the world today:

_____

One thing I learned about myself today:

_____

One thing I will do different tomorrow:

_____

General thoughts about today:

_____

_____

_____

DATE: _____ **PLACE:** _____ **BUDGET:** _____

---◆---

3 things I did today:

01. _____

02. _____

03. _____

Favorite thing I ate today:

_____

One person I met today (name, age, where they are from):

_____

One thing I learned about the world today:

_____

One thing I learned about myself today:

_____

One thing I will do different tomorrow:

_____

General thoughts about today:

_____

_____

_____

DATE: _____ **PLACE:** _____ **BUDGET:** _____

"Once a year, go someplace you've never been before."
— Dalai Lama

3 things I did today:

01. _____

02. _____

03. _____

Favorite thing I ate today:

_____

One person I met today (name, age, where they are from):

_____

One thing I learned about the world today:

_____

One thing I learned about myself today:

_____

One thing I will do different tomorrow:

_____

General thoughts about today:

_____

_____

_____

DATE: _____   **PLACE:** _____   **BUDGET:** _____

---✦---

3 things I did today:

01. _____ ____

02. _____

03. _____

Favorite thing I ate today:

_____

One person I met today (name, age, where they are from):

_____

One thing I learned about the world today:

_____

One thing I learned about myself today:

_____

One thing I will do different tomorrow:

_____

General thoughts about today:

_____

_____

_____

DATE: _____ PLACE: _____ BUDGET: _____

"It is not the destination where you end up but the mishaps and memories you
create along the way!" — Penelope Riley

3 things I did today:

01. _____

02. _____

03. _____

Favorite thing I ate today:

_____

One person I met today (name, age, where they are from):

_____

One thing I learned about the world today:

_____

One thing I learned about myself today:

_____

One thing I will do different tomorrow:

_____

General thoughts about today:

_____

_____

_____

DATE: _____ **PLACE:** _____ **BUDGET:** _____

---✦---

3 things I did today:

01. _____ _____

02. _____

03. _____

Favorite thing I ate today:

_____

One person I met today (name, age, where they are from):

_____

One thing I learned about the world today:

_____

One thing I learned about myself today:

_____

One thing I will do different tomorrow:

_____

General thoughts about today:

_____

_____

_____

DATE: _____   **PLACE:** _____   **BUDGET:** _____

"The world is a book and those who do not travel read only a page."
— Saint Augustine

3 things I did today:

01. _____

02. _____

03. _____

Favorite thing I ate today:

_____

One person I met today (name, age, where they are from):

_____

One thing I learned about the world today:

_____

One thing I learned about myself today:

_____

One thing I will do different tomorrow:

_____

General thoughts about today:

_____

_____

_____

DATE: _____ **PLACE:** _____ **BUDGET:** _____

---✦---

3 things I did today:

01. _____

02. _____

03. _____

Favorite thing I ate today:

_____

One person I met today (name, age, where they are from):

_____

One thing I learned about the world today:

_____

One thing I learned about myself today:

_____

One thing I will do different tomorrow:

_____

General thoughts about today:

_____

_____

_____

DATE: _____ **PLACE:** _____ **BUDGET:** _____

"Since life is short and the world is wide, the sooner you start exploring it, the better."
— Simon Raven

3 things I did today:

01. _____

02. _____

03. _____

Favorite thing I ate today:

_____

One person I met today (name, age, where they are from):

_____

One thing I learned about the world today:

_____

One thing I learned about myself today:

_____

One thing I will do different tomorrow:

_____

General thoughts about today:

_____

_____

_____

DATE: _____ **PLACE:** _____ **BUDGET:** _____

———————————— ✦ ————————————

3 things I did today:

01. _____ __

02. _____

03. _____

Favorite thing I ate today:

_____

One person I met today (name, age, where they are from):

_____

One thing I learned about the world today:

_____

One thing I learned about myself today:

_____

One thing I will do different tomorrow:

_____

General thoughts about today:

_____

_____

_____

DATE: _____ **PLACE:** _____ **BUDGET:** _____

"To my mind, the greatest reward and luxury of travel is to be able to experience everyday things as if for the first time." — Bill Bryson

3 things I did today:

01. _____

02. _____

03. _____

Favorite thing I ate today:

_____

One person I met today (name, age, where they are from):

_____

One thing I learned about the world today:

_____

One thing I learned about myself today:

_____

One thing I will do different tomorrow:

_____

General thoughts about today:

_____

_____

_____

DATE: _____ **PLACE:** _____ **BUDGET:** _____

———————◈———————

3 things I did today:

01. _____

02. _____

03. _____

Favorite thing I ate today:

_____

One person I met today (name, age, where they are from):

_____

One thing I learned about the world today:

_____

One thing I learned about myself today:

_____

One thing I will do different tomorrow:

_____

General thoughts about today:

_____

_____

_____

DATE: _____   **PLACE:** _____   **BUDGET:** _____

"It is not down in any map; true places never are."
— Herman Melville

3 things I did today:

01. _____

02. _____

03. _____

Favorite thing I ate today:

_____

One person I met today (name, age, where they are from):

_____

One thing I learned about the world today:

_____

One thing I learned about myself today:

_____

One thing I will do different tomorrow:

_____

General thoughts about today:

_____

_____

_____

DATE: _____   **PLACE:** _____   **BUDGET:** _____

———————————— ✦ ————————————

3 things I did today:

01. _____

02. _____

03. _____

Favorite thing I ate today:

_____

One person I met today (name, age, where they are from):

_____

One thing I learned about the world today:

_____

One thing I learned about myself today:

_____

One thing I will do different tomorrow:

_____

General thoughts about today:

_____

_____

_____

DATE: _____ **PLACE:** _____ **BUDGET:** _____

"Though we travel the world over to find the beautiful, we must carry it with us or we find it not." — Ralph Waldo Emerson

3 things I did today:

01. _____

02. _____

03. _____

Favorite thing I ate today:

_____

One person I met today (name, age, where they are from):

_____

One thing I learned about the world today:

_____

One thing I learned about myself today:

_____

One thing I will do different tomorrow:

_____

General thoughts about today:

_____

_____

_____

DATE: _____   **PLACE:** _____   **BUDGET:** _____

———————— ✦ ————————

3 things I did today:

01. _____

02. _____

03. _____

Favorite thing I ate today:

_____

One person I met today (name, age, where they are from):

_____

One thing I learned about the world today:

_____

One thing I learned about myself today:

_____

One thing I will do different tomorrow:

_____

General thoughts about today:

_____

_____

_____

DATE: _____ **PLACE:** _____ **BUDGET:** _____

"A good traveler has no fixed plans, and is not intent on arriving."
— Lao Tzu

3 things I did today:

01. _____

02. _____

03. _____

Favorite thing I ate today:

_____

One person I met today (name, age, where they are from):

_____

One thing I learned about the world today:

_____

One thing I learned about myself today:

_____

One thing I will do different tomorrow:

_____

General thoughts about today:

_____

_____

_____

DATE: _____ **PLACE:** _____ **BUDGET:** _____

———————— ✦ ————————

3 things I did today:

01. _____ ____

02. _____

03. _____

Favorite thing I ate today:

_____

One person I met today (name, age, where they are from):

_____

One thing I learned about the world today:

_____

One thing I learned about myself today:

_____

One thing I will do different tomorrow:

_____

General thoughts about today:

_____

_____

_____

DATE: _____   **PLACE:** _____   **BUDGET:** _____

"There is something about the momentum of travel that makes you want to just keep moving, to never stop." — Bill Bryson

3 things I did today:

01. _____

02. _____

03. _____

Favorite thing I ate today:

_____

One person I met today (name, age, where they are from):

_____

One thing I learned about the world today:

_____

One thing I learned about myself today:

_____

One thing I will do different tomorrow:

_____

General thoughts about today:

_____

_____

_____

DATE: _____   **PLACE:** _____   **BUDGET:** _____

---------- ✦ ----------

3 things I did today:

01. _____

02. _____

03. _____

Favorite thing I ate today:

_____

One person I met today (name, age, where they are from):

_____

One thing I learned about the world today:

_____

One thing I learned about myself today:

_____

One thing I will do different tomorrow:

_____

General thoughts about today:

_____

_____

_____

DATE: _____   **PLACE:** _____   **BUDGET:** _____

"A great way to learn about your country is to leave it."
— Henry Rollins

3 things I did today:

01. _____

02. _____

03. _____

Favorite thing I ate today:

_____

One person I met today (name, age, where they are from):

_____

One thing I learned about the world today:

_____

One thing I learned about myself today:

_____

One thing I will do different tomorrow:

_____

General thoughts about today:

_____

_____

_____

DATE: _____ **PLACE:** _____ **BUDGET:** _____

———————◈———————

3 things I did today:

01. _____ __

02. _____

03. _____

Favorite thing I ate today:

_____

One person I met today (name, age, where they are from):

_____

One thing I learned about the world today:

_____

One thing I learned about myself today:

_____

One thing I will do different tomorrow:

_____

General thoughts about today:

_____

_____

_____

"If happiness is the goal– and it should be, then adventures should be a priority."
— Richard Branson

3 things I did today:

01. _____

02. _____

03. _____

Favorite thing I ate today:

_____

One person I met today (name, age, where they are from):

_____

One thing I learned about the world today:

_____

One thing I learned about myself today:

_____

One thing I will do different tomorrow:

_____

General thoughts about today:

_____

_____

_____

DATE: _____ **PLACE:** _____ **BUDGET:** _____

———————————— ✦ ————————————

3 things I did today:

01. _____

02. _____

03. _____

Favorite thing I ate today:

_____

One person I met today (name, age, where they are from):

_____

One thing I learned about the world today:

_____

One thing I learned about myself today:

_____

One thing I will do different tomorrow:

_____

General thoughts about today:

_____

_____

_____

DATE: _____   **PLACE:** _____   **BUDGET:** _____

"You are never too old to set another goal or to dream a new dream."
— Les Brown

3 things I did today:

01. _____

02. _____

03. _____

Favorite thing I ate today:

_____

One person I met today (name, age, where they are from):

_____

One thing I learned about the world today:

_____

One thing I learned about myself today:

_____

One thing I will do different tomorrow:

_____

General thoughts about today:

_____

_____

_____

———————— ✦ ————————

3 things I did today:

01. _____ ____

02. _____

03. _____

Favorite thing I ate today:

_____

One person I met today (name, age, where they are from):

_____

One thing I learned about the world today:

_____

One thing I learned about myself today:

_____

One thing I will do different tomorrow:

_____

General thoughts about today:

_____

_____

_____

DATE: _____   PLACE: _____   BUDGET: _____

"Wherever my travels may lead, paradise is where I am."
— Voltaire

3 things I did today:

01. _____

02. _____

03. _____

Favorite thing I ate today:

_____

One person I met today (name, age, where they are from):

_____

One thing I learned about the world today:

_____

One thing I learned about myself today:

_____

One thing I will do different tomorrow:

_____

General thoughts about today:

_____

_____

_____

DATE: _____   **PLACE:** _____   **BUDGET:** _____

---

3 things I did today:

01. _____

02. _____

03. _____

Favorite thing I ate today:

_____

One person I met today (name, age, where they are from):

_____

One thing I learned about the world today:

_____

One thing I learned about myself today:

_____

One thing I will do different tomorrow:

_____

General thoughts about today:

_____

_____

_____

DATE: _____ **PLACE:** _____ **BUDGET:** _____

"The most beautiful in the world is, of course, the world itself."
— Wallace Stevens

3 things I did today:

01. _____

02. _____

03. _____

Favorite thing I ate today:

_____

One person I met today (name, age, where they are from):

_____

One thing I learned about the world today:

_____

One thing I learned about myself today:

_____

One thing I will do different tomorrow:

_____

General thoughts about today:

_____

_____

_____

DATE: _____ **PLACE:** _____ **BUDGET:** _____

———————— ✦ ————————

3 things I did today:

01. _____

02. _____

03. _____

Favorite thing I ate today:

_____

One person I met today (name, age, where they are from):

_____

One thing I learned about the world today:

_____

One thing I learned about myself today:

_____

One thing I will do different tomorrow:

_____

General thoughts about today:

_____

_____

_____

DATE: _____   **PLACE:** _____   **BUDGET:** _____

"We are what we repeatedly do. Excellence, then, is not an act, but a habit."
— William Durant

3 things I did today:

01. _____

02. _____

03. _____

Favorite thing I ate today:

_____

One person I met today (name, age, where they are from):

_____

One thing I learned about the world today:

_____

One thing I learned about myself today:

_____

One thing I will do different tomorrow:

_____

General thoughts about today:

_____

_____

_____

DATE: _____ **PLACE:** _____ **BUDGET:** _____

---✦---

3 things I did today:

01. _____

02. _____

03. _____

Favorite thing I ate today:

_____

One person I met today (name, age, where they are from):

_____

One thing I learned about the world today:

_____

One thing I learned about myself today:

_____

One thing I will do different tomorrow:

_____

General thoughts about today:

_____

_____

_____

DATE: _____   **PLACE:** _____   **BUDGET:** _____

"Not all those who wander are lost."
— J.R.R. Tolkien

3 things I did today:

01. _____

02. _____

03. _____

Favorite thing I ate today:

_____

One person I met today (name, age, where they are from):

_____

One thing I learned about the world today:

_____

One thing I learned about myself today:

_____

One thing I will do different tomorrow:

_____

General thoughts about today:

_____

_____

_____

DATE: _____ **PLACE:** _____ **BUDGET:** _____

---◆---

3 things I did today:

01. _____

02. _____

03. _____

Favorite thing I ate today:

_____

One person I met today (name, age, where they are from):

_____

One thing I learned about the world today:

_____

One thing I learned about myself today:

_____

One thing I will do different tomorrow:

_____

General thoughts about today:

_____

_____

_____

DATE: _____ **PLACE:** _____ **BUDGET:** _____

"Like all great travellers, I have seen more than I remember and remember more than I have seen." — Benjamin Disraeli

3 things I did today:

01. _____

02. _____

03. _____

Favorite thing I ate today:

_____

One person I met today (name, age, where they are from):

_____

One thing I learned about the world today:

_____

One thing I learned about myself today:

_____

One thing I will do different tomorrow:

_____

General thoughts about today:

_____

_____

_____

DATE: _____ **PLACE:** _____ **BUDGET:** _____

———————◈———————

3 things I did today:

01. _____

02. _____

03. _____

Favorite thing I ate today:

_____

One person I met today (name, age, where they are from):

_____

One thing I learned about the world today:

_____

One thing I learned about myself today:

_____

One thing I will do different tomorrow:

_____

General thoughts about today:

_____

_____

_____

DATE: _____ **PLACE:** _____ **BUDGET:** _____

"A mind that is stretched by a new experience can never go back to its old dimensions." — Oliver Wendell Holmes

3 things I did today:

01. _____

02. _____

03. _____

Favorite thing I ate today:

_____

One person I met today (name, age, where they are from):

_____

One thing I learned about the world today:

_____

One thing I learned about myself today:

_____

One thing I will do different tomorrow:

_____

General thoughts about today:

_____

_____

_____

DATE: _____ **PLACE:** _____ **BUDGET:** _____

3 things I did today:

01. _____

02. _____

03. _____

Favorite thing I ate today:

_____

One person I met today (name, age, where they are from):

_____

One thing I learned about the world today:

_____

One thing I learned about myself today:

_____

One thing I will do different tomorrow:

_____

General thoughts about today:

_____

_____

_____

DATE: _____ **PLACE:** _____ **BUDGET:** _____

"Travel, at its best, transforms us in ways that aren't always apparent until we're back home." — Eric Weiner

3 things I did today:

01. _____

02. _____

03. _____

Favorite thing I ate today:

_____

One person I met today (name, age, where they are from):

_____

One thing I learned about the world today:

_____

One thing I learned about myself today:

_____

One thing I will do different tomorrow:

_____

General thoughts about today:

_____

_____

_____

DATE: _____ PLACE: _____ BUDGET: _____

---------------------◆---------------------

3 things I did today:

01. _____

02. _____

03. _____

Favorite thing I ate today:

_____

One person I met today (name, age, where they are from):

_____

One thing I learned about the world today:

_____

One thing I learned about myself today:

_____

One thing I will do different tomorrow:

_____

General thoughts about today:

_____

_____

_____

DATE: _____ **PLACE:** _____ **BUDGET:** _____

"When it is obvious that goals can't be reached, don't adjust the goals, but adjust the action steps." — Confucius

3 things I did today:

01. _____

02. _____

03. _____

Favorite thing I ate today:

_____

One person I met today (name, age, where they are from):

_____

One thing I learned about the world today:

_____

One thing I learned about myself today:

_____

One thing I will do different tomorrow:

_____

General thoughts about today:

_____

_____

_____

DATE: _____ PLACE: _____ BUDGET: _____

———————————◆———————————

3 things I did today:

01. _____

02. _____

03. _____

Favorite thing I ate today:

_____

One person I met today (name, age, where they are from):

_____

One thing I learned about the world today:

_____

One thing I learned about myself today:

_____

One thing I will do different tomorrow:

_____

General thoughts about today:

_____

_____

_____

DATE: _____   **PLACE:** _____   **BUDGET:** _____

"The real voyage of discovery consists not in seeking new landscapes, but in having new eyes." — Marcel Proust

3 things I did today:

01. _____

02. _____

03. _____

Favorite thing I ate today:

_____

One person I met today (name, age, where they are from):

_____

One thing I learned about the world today:

_____

One thing I learned about myself today:

_____

One thing I will do different tomorrow:

_____

General thoughts about today:

_____

_____

_____

DATE: _____ **PLACE:** _____ **BUDGET:** _____

———————— ✦ ————————

3 things I did today:

01. _____

02. _____

03. _____

Favorite thing I ate today:

_____

One person I met today (name, age, where they are from):

_____

One thing I learned about the world today:

_____

One thing I learned about myself today:

_____

One thing I will do different tomorrow:

_____

General thoughts about today:

_____

_____

_____

DATE: _____   **PLACE:** _____   **BUDGET:** _____

"The world is big and I want to have a good look at it before it gets dark."
— John Muir

3 things I did today:

01. _____

02. _____

03. _____

Favorite thing I ate today:

_____

One person I met today (name, age, where they are from):

_____

One thing I learned about the world today:

_____

One thing I learned about myself today:

_____

One thing I will do different tomorrow:

_____

General thoughts about today:

_____

_____

_____

DATE: _____ **PLACE:** _____ **BUDGET:** _____

---✦---

3 things I did today:

01. _____

02. _____

03. _____

Favorite thing I ate today:

_____

One person I met today (name, age, where they are from):

_____

One thing I learned about the world today:

_____

One thing I learned about myself today:

_____

One thing I will do different tomorrow:

_____

General thoughts about today:

_____

_____

_____

"Traveling is like flirting with life. It's like saying, 'I would stay and love you, but I
have to go; this is my station.'" — Lisa St. Aubin de Teran

3 things I did today:

01. _____

02. _____

03. _____

Favorite thing I ate today:

_____

One person I met today (name, age, where they are from):

_____

One thing I learned about the world today:

_____

One thing I learned about myself today:

_____

One thing I will do different tomorrow:

_____

General thoughts about today:

_____

_____

_____

DATE: _____ **PLACE:** _____ **BUDGET:** _____

---✦---

3 things I did today:

01. _____

02. _____

03. _____

Favorite thing I ate today:

_____

One person I met today (name, age, where they are from):

_____

One thing I learned about the world today:

_____

One thing I learned about myself today:

_____

One thing I will do different tomorrow:

_____

General thoughts about today:

_____

_____

_____

DATE: _____   PLACE: _____   BUDGET: _____

"Loneliness adds beauty to life. It puts a special burn on sunsets and makes night air smell better." — Henry Rollins

3 things I did today:

01. _____

02. _____

03. _____

Favorite thing I ate today:

_____

One person I met today (name, age, where they are from):

_____

One thing I learned about the world today:

_____

One thing I learned about myself today:

_____

One thing I will do different tomorrow:

_____

General thoughts about today:

_____

_____

_____

DATE: _____   **PLACE:** _____   **BUDGET:** _____

———————————◈———————————

3 things I did today:

01. _____

02. _____

03. _____

Favorite thing I ate today:

_____

One person I met today (name, age, where they are from):

_____

One thing I learned about the world today:

_____

One thing I learned about myself today:

_____

One thing I will do different tomorrow:

_____

General thoughts about today:

_____

_____

_____

DATE: _____ **PLACE:** _____ **BUDGET:** _____

"Be fearless in the pursuit of what sets your soul on fire."
— Jennifer Lee

3 things I did today:

01. _____

02. _____

03. _____

Favorite thing I ate today:

_____

One person I met today (name, age, where they are from):

_____

One thing I learned about the world today:

_____

One thing I learned about myself today:

_____

One thing I will do different tomorrow:

_____

General thoughts about today:

_____

_____

_____

DATE: _____   **PLACE:** _____   **BUDGET:** _____

———————◆———————

3 things I did today:

01. _____

02. _____

03. _____

Favorite thing I ate today:

_____

One person I met today (name, age, where they are from):

_____

One thing I learned about the world today:

_____

One thing I learned about myself today:

_____

One thing I will do different tomorrow:

_____

General thoughts about today:

_____

_____

_____

DATE: _____   **PLACE:** _____   **BUDGET:** _____

"Our happiest moments as tourists always seem to come when we stumble upon one thing while in pursuit of something else." — Lawrence Block

3 things I did today:

01. _____

02. _____

03. _____

Favorite thing I ate today:

_____

One person I met today (name, age, where they are from):

_____

One thing I learned about the world today:

_____

One thing I learned about myself today:

_____

One thing I will do different tomorrow:

_____

General thoughts about today:

_____

_____

_____

DATE: _____   **PLACE:** _____   **BUDGET:** _____

---✦---

3 things I did today:

01. _____

02. _____

03. _____

Favorite thing I ate today:

_____

One person I met today (name, age, where they are from):

_____

One thing I learned about the world today:

_____

One thing I learned about myself today:

_____

One thing I will do different tomorrow:

_____

General thoughts about today:

_____

_____

_____

DATE: _____ **PLACE:** _____ **BUDGET:** _____

"The healthiest response to life is joy."
— Deepak Chopra

3 things I did today:

01. _____

02. _____

03. _____

Favorite thing I ate today:

_____

One person I met today (name, age, where they are from):

_____

One thing I learned about the world today:

_____

One thing I learned about myself today:

_____

One thing I will do different tomorrow:

_____

General thoughts about today:

_____

_____

_____

DATE: _____ **PLACE:** _____ **BUDGET:** _____

---- ✧ ----

3 things I did today:

01. _____

02. _____

03. _____

Favorite thing I ate today:

_____

One person I met today (name, age, where they are from):

_____

One thing I learned about the world today:

_____

One thing I learned about myself today:

_____

One thing I will do different tomorrow:

_____

General thoughts about today:

_____

_____

_____

DATE: _____   PLACE: _____   BUDGET: _____

"You have power over your mind – not outside events. Realize this, and you will find strength." — Marcus Aurelius

3 things I did today:

01. _____

02. _____

03. _____

Favorite thing I ate today:

_____

One person I met today (name, age, where they are from):

_____

One thing I learned about the world today:

_____

One thing I learned about myself today:

_____

One thing I will do different tomorrow:

_____

General thoughts about today:

_____

_____

_____

DATE: _____ **PLACE:** _____ **BUDGET:** _____

———————— ✦ ————————

3 things I did today:

01. _____

02. _____

03. _____

Favorite thing I ate today:

_____

One person I met today (name, age, where they are from):

_____

One thing I learned about the world today:

_____

One thing I learned about myself today:

_____

One thing I will do different tomorrow:

_____

General thoughts about today:

_____

_____

_____

DATE: _____   **PLACE:** _____   **BUDGET:** _____

"To awaken quite alone in a strange town is one of the pleasantest sensations in the world." — Freya Stark

3 things I did today:

01. _____

02. _____

03. _____

Favorite thing I ate today:

_____

One person I met today (name, age, where they are from):

_____

One thing I learned about the world today:

_____

One thing I learned about myself today:

_____

One thing I will do different tomorrow:

_____

General thoughts about today:

_____

_____

_____

DATE: _____   **PLACE:** _____   **BUDGET:** _____

----------------◈----------------

3 things I did today:

01. _____

02. _____

03. _____

Favorite thing I ate today:

_____

One person I met today (name, age, where they are from):

_____

One thing I learned about the world today:

_____

One thing I learned about myself today:

_____

One thing I will do different tomorrow:

_____

General thoughts about today:

_____

_____

_____

DATE: _____   **PLACE:** _____   **BUDGET:** _____

"When people ask me why I still have hope and energy after all these years,
I always say: Because I travel." — Gloria Steinem

3 things I did today:

01. _____

02. _____

03. _____

Favorite thing I ate today:

_____

One person I met today (name, age, where they are from):

_____

One thing I learned about the world today:

_____

One thing I learned about myself today:

_____

One thing I will do different tomorrow:

_____

General thoughts about today:

_____

_____

_____

DATE: _____   **PLACE:** _____   **BUDGET:** _____

---

3 things I did today:

01. _____

02. _____

03. _____

Favorite thing I ate today:

_____

One person I met today (name, age, where they are from):

_____

One thing I learned about the world today:

_____

One thing I learned about myself today:

_____

One thing I will do different tomorrow:

_____

General thoughts about today:

_____

_____

_____

DATE: _____   **PLACE:** _____   **BUDGET:** _____

"Take every chance you get in life, because some things only happen once."
— Karen Gibbs

3 things I did today:

01. _____

02. _____

03. _____

Favorite thing I ate today:

_____

One person I met today (name, age, where they are from):

_____

One thing I learned about the world today:

_____

One thing I learned about myself today:

_____

One thing I will do different tomorrow:

_____

General thoughts about today:

_____

_____

_____

DATE: _____ **PLACE:** _____ **BUDGET:** _____

---✦---

3 things I did today:

01. _____

02. _____

03. _____

Favorite thing I ate today:

_____

One person I met today (name, age, where they are from):

_____

One thing I learned about the world today:

_____

One thing I learned about myself today:

_____

One thing I will do different tomorrow:

_____

General thoughts about today:

_____

_____

_____

DATE: _____   **PLACE:** _____   **BUDGET:** _____

"Life is not a problem to be solved, but a reality to be experienced."
— Søren Kierkegaard

3 things I did today:

01. _____

02. _____

03. _____

Favorite thing I ate today:

_____

One person I met today (name, age, where they are from):

_____

One thing I learned about the world today:

_____

One thing I learned about myself today:

_____

One thing I will do different tomorrow:

_____

General thoughts about today:

_____

_____

_____

───────────── ✦ ─────────────

3 things I did today:

01. _____

02. _____

03. _____

Favorite thing I ate today:

_____

One person I met today (name, age, where they are from):

_____

One thing I learned about the world today:

_____

One thing I learned about myself today:

_____

One thing I will do different tomorrow:

_____

General thoughts about today:

_____

_____

_____

DATE: _____   **PLACE:** _____   **BUDGET:** _____

"Go confidently in the direction of your dreams! Live the life you've imagined."
— Henry David Thoreau

3 things I did today:

01. _____

02. _____

03. _____

Favorite thing I ate today:

_____

One person I met today (name, age, where they are from):

_____

One thing I learned about the world today:

_____

One thing I learned about myself today:

_____

One thing I will do different tomorrow:

_____

General thoughts about today:

_____

_____

_____

DATE: _____   **PLACE:** _____   **BUDGET:** _____

—————————— ✦ ——————————

3 things I did today:

01. _____

02. _____

03. _____

Favorite thing I ate today:

_____

One person I met today (name, age, where they are from):

_____

One thing I learned about the world today:

_____

One thing I learned about myself today:

_____

One thing I will do different tomorrow:

_____

General thoughts about today:

_____

_____

_____

DATE: _____   **PLACE:** _____   **BUDGET:** _____

"One's destination is never a place, but a new way of seeing things."
— Henry Miller

3 things I did today:

01. _____

02. _____

03. _____

Favorite thing I ate today:

_____

One person I met today (name, age, where they are from):

_____

One thing I learned about the world today:

_____

One thing I learned about myself today:

_____

One thing I will do different tomorrow:

_____

General thoughts about today:

_____

_____

_____

DATE: _____ **PLACE:** _____ **BUDGET:** _____

_____ ✦ _____

3 things I did today:

01. _____

02. _____

03. _____

Favorite thing I ate today:

_____

One person I met today (name, age, where they are from):

_____

One thing I learned about the world today:

_____

One thing I learned about myself today:

_____

One thing I will do different tomorrow:

_____

General thoughts about today:

_____

_____

_____

DATE: _____   PLACE: _____   BUDGET: _____

"Not until we are lost do we begin to find ourselves."
— Henry David Thoreau

3 things I did today:

01. _____

02. _____

03. _____

Favorite thing I ate today:

_____

One person I met today (name, age, where they are from):

_____

One thing I learned about the world today:

_____

One thing I learned about myself today:

_____

One thing I will do different tomorrow:

_____

General thoughts about today:

_____

_____

_____

DATE: _____ **PLACE:** _____ **BUDGET:** _____

---

3 things I did today:

01. _____

02. _____

03. _____

Favorite thing I ate today:

_____

One person I met today (name, age, where they are from):

_____

One thing I learned about the world today:

_____

One thing I learned about myself today:

_____

One thing I will do different tomorrow:

_____

General thoughts about today:

_____

_____

_____

DATE: _____   **PLACE:** _____   **BUDGET:** _____

"We wander for distraction but we travel for fulfillment."
— Hilaire Belloc

3 things I did today:

01. _____

02. _____

03. _____

Favorite thing I ate today:

_____

One person I met today (name, age, where they are from):

_____

One thing I learned about the world today:

_____

One thing I learned about myself today:

_____

One thing I will do different tomorrow:

_____

General thoughts about today:

_____

_____

_____

DATE: _____ **PLACE:** _____ **BUDGET:** _____

———————————◈———————————

3 things I did today:

01. _____

02. _____

03. _____

Favorite thing I ate today:

_____

One person I met today (name, age, where they are from):

_____

One thing I learned about the world today:

_____

One thing I learned about myself today:

_____

One thing I will do different tomorrow:

_____

General thoughts about today:

_____

_____

_____

DATE: _____   **PLACE:** _____   **BUDGET:** _____

"If you think adventure is dangerous, try routine, it's lethal."
— Paulo Coelho

3 things I did today:

01. _____

02. _____

03. _____

Favorite thing I ate today:

_____

One person I met today (name, age, where they are from):

_____

One thing I learned about the world today:

_____

One thing I learned about myself today:

_____

One thing I will do different tomorrow:

_____

General thoughts about today:

_____

_____

_____

DATE: _____   **PLACE:** _____   **BUDGET:** _____

───────────────◆───────────────

3 things I did today:

01. _____

02. _____

03. _____

Favorite thing I ate today:

_____

One person I met today (name, age, where they are from):

_____

One thing I learned about the world today:

_____

One thing I learned about myself today:

_____

One thing I will do different tomorrow:

_____

General thoughts about today:

_____

_____

_____

DATE: _____ PLACE: _____ BUDGET: _____

"An inconvenience is an adventure wrongly considered."
— Gilbert K. Chesterton

3 things I did today:

01. _____

02. _____

03. _____

Favorite thing I ate today:

_____

One person I met today (name, age, where they are from):

_____

One thing I learned about the world today:

_____

One thing I learned about myself today:

_____

One thing I will do different tomorrow:

_____

General thoughts about today:

_____

_____

_____

DATE: _____ **PLACE:** _____ **BUDGET:** _____

———————— ✦ ————————

3 things I did today:

01. _____

02. _____

03. _____

Favorite thing I ate today:

_____

One person I met today (name, age, where they are from):

_____

One thing I learned about the world today:

_____

One thing I learned about myself today:

_____

One thing I will do different tomorrow:

_____

General thoughts about today:

_____

_____

_____

DATE: _____   **PLACE:** _____   **BUDGET:** _____

"I travel not to cross countries off a list, but to ignite passionate affairs
with destinations." — Nyssa P. Chopra

3 things I did today:

01. _____

02. _____

03. _____

Favorite thing I ate today:

_____

One person I met today (name, age, where they are from):

_____

One thing I learned about the world today:

_____

One thing I learned about myself today:

_____

One thing I will do different tomorrow:

_____

General thoughts about today:

_____

_____

_____

DATE: _____   **PLACE:** _____   **BUDGET:** _____

---

3 things I did today:

01. _____

02. _____

03. _____

Favorite thing I ate today:

_____

One person I met today (name, age, where they are from):

_____

One thing I learned about the world today:

_____

One thing I learned about myself today:

_____

One thing I will do different tomorrow:

_____

General thoughts about today:

_____

_____

_____

DATE: _____   **PLACE:** _____   **BUDGET:** _____

"All you've got to do is decide to go and the hardest part is over."
— Tony Wheeler

3 things I did today:

01. _____

02. _____

03. _____

Favorite thing I ate today:

_____

One person I met today (name, age, where they are from):

_____

One thing I learned about the world today:

_____

One thing I learned about myself today:

_____

One thing I will do different tomorrow:

_____

General thoughts about today:

_____

_____

_____

DATE: _____ **PLACE:** _____ **BUDGET:** _____

———————————◆———————————

3 things I did today:

01. _____

02. _____

03. _____

Favorite thing I ate today:

_____

One person I met today (name, age, where they are from):

_____

One thing I learned about the world today:

_____

One thing I learned about myself today:

_____

One thing I will do different tomorrow:

_____

General thoughts about today:

_____

_____

_____

DATE: _____ **PLACE:** _____ **BUDGET:** _____

"It is better to travel well than to arrive."
— Unknown

3 things I did today:

01. _____

02. _____

03. _____

Favorite thing I ate today:

_____

One person I met today (name, age, where they are from):

_____

One thing I learned about the world today:

_____

One thing I learned about myself today:

_____

One thing I will do different tomorrow:

_____

General thoughts about today:

_____

_____

_____

DATE: _____ **PLACE:** _____ **BUDGET:** _____

———————————— ✦ ————————————

3 things I did today:

01. _____

02. _____

03. _____

Favorite thing I ate today:

_____

One person I met today (name, age, where they are from):

_____

One thing I learned about the world today:

_____

One thing I learned about myself today:

_____

One thing I will do different tomorrow:

_____

General thoughts about today:

_____

_____

_____

DATE: _____ **PLACE:** _____ **BUDGET:** _____

"Time flies. It's up to you to be the navigator."
— Robert Orben

3 things I did today:

01. _____

02. _____

03. _____

Favorite thing I ate today:

_____

One person I met today (name, age, where they are from):

_____

One thing I learned about the world today:

_____

One thing I learned about myself today:

_____

One thing I will do different tomorrow:

_____

General thoughts about today:

_____

_____

_____

DATE: _____   **PLACE:** _____   **BUDGET:** _____

———————————— ✦ ————————————

3 things I did today:

01. _____

02. _____

03. _____

Favorite thing I ate today:

_____

One person I met today (name, age, where they are from):

_____

One thing I learned about the world today:

_____

One thing I learned about myself today:

_____

One thing I will do different tomorrow:

_____

General thoughts about today:

_____

_____

_____

DATE: _____ **PLACE:** _____ **BUDGET:** _____

"Art and love are the same thing: It's the process of seeing yourself in things that are not you." — Chuck Klosterman

3 things I did today:

01. _____

02. _____

03. _____

Favorite thing I ate today:

_____

One person I met today (name, age, where they are from):

_____

One thing I learned about the world today:

_____

One thing I learned about myself today:

_____

One thing I will do different tomorrow:

_____

General thoughts about today:

_____

_____

_____

DATE: _____ PLACE: _____ BUDGET: _____

———————————— ✦ ————————————

3 things I did today:

01. _____

02. _____

03. _____

Favorite thing I ate today:

_____

One person I met today (name, age, where they are from):

_____

One thing I learned about the world today:

_____

One thing I learned about myself today:

_____

One thing I will do different tomorrow:

_____

General thoughts about today:

_____

_____

_____

DATE: _____ **PLACE:** _____ **BUDGET:** _____

"When you're traveling, you are what you are right there and then. People don't have your past to hold against you." — William Least Heat Moon

3 things I did today:

01. _____

02. _____

03. _____

Favorite thing I ate today:

_____

One person I met today (name, age, where they are from):

_____

One thing I learned about the world today:

_____

One thing I learned about myself today:

_____

One thing I will do different tomorrow:

_____

General thoughts about today:

_____

_____

_____

DATE: _____   **PLACE:** _____   **BUDGET:** _____

3 things I did today:

01. _____

02. _____

03. _____

Favorite thing I ate today:

_____

One person I met today (name, age, where they are from):

_____

One thing I learned about the world today:

_____

One thing I learned about myself today:

_____

One thing I will do different tomorrow:

_____

General thoughts about today:

_____

_____

_____

DATE: _____   **PLACE:** _____   **BUDGET:** _____

"The best view comes after the hardest climb."
— Unknown

3 things I did today:

01. _____

02. _____

03. _____

Favorite thing I ate today:

_____

One person I met today (name, age, where they are from):

_____

One thing I learned about the world today:

_____

One thing I learned about myself today:

_____

One thing I will do different tomorrow:

_____

General thoughts about today:

_____

_____

_____

DATE: _____ **PLACE:** _____ **BUDGET:** _____

————————————◆————————————

3 things I did today:

01. _____

02. _____

03. _____

Favorite thing I ate today:

_____

One person I met today (name, age, where they are from):

_____

One thing I learned about the world today:

_____

One thing I learned about myself today:

_____

One thing I will do different tomorrow:

_____

General thoughts about today:

_____

_____

_____

DATE: _____ **PLACE:** _____ **BUDGET:** _____

3 things I did today:

01. _____

02. _____

03. _____

Favorite thing I ate today:

_____

One person I met today (name, age, where they are from):

_____

One thing I learned about the world today:

_____

One thing I learned about myself today:

_____

One thing I will do different tomorrow:

_____

General thoughts about today:

_____

_____

_____

DATE: _____ **PLACE:** _____ **BUDGET:** _____

———————————— ✦ ————————————

3 things I did today:

01. _____

02. _____

03. _____

Favorite thing I ate today:

_____

One person I met today (name, age, where they are from):

_____

One thing I learned about the world today:

_____

One thing I learned about myself today:

_____

One thing I will do different tomorrow:

_____

General thoughts about today:

_____

_____

_____

DATE: _____   **PLACE:** _____   **BUDGET:** _____

"A nomad I will remain for life, in love with distant and uncharted places."
— Isabelle Eberhardt

3 things I did today:

01. _____

02. _____

03. _____

Favorite thing I ate today:

_____

One person I met today (name, age, where they are from):

_____

One thing I learned about the world today:

_____

One thing I learned about myself today:

_____

One thing I will do different tomorrow:

_____

General thoughts about today:

_____

_____

_____

DATE: _____ **PLACE:** _____ **BUDGET:** _____

---❖---

3 things I did today:

01. _____

02. _____

03. _____

Favorite thing I ate today:

_____

One person I met today (name, age, where they are from):

_____

One thing I learned about the world today:

_____

One thing I learned about myself today:

_____

One thing I will do different tomorrow:

_____

General thoughts about today:

_____

_____

_____

DATE: _____ **PLACE:** _____ **BUDGET:** _____

"A life is not important except in the impact it has on other lives."
— Jackie Robinson

3 things I did today:

01. _____

02. _____

03. _____

Favorite thing I ate today:

_____

One person I met today (name, age, where they are from):

_____

One thing I learned about the world today:

_____

One thing I learned about myself today:

_____

One thing I will do different tomorrow:

_____

General thoughts about today:

_____

_____

_____

DATE: _____ **PLACE:** _____ **BUDGET:** _____

---------------- ✦ ----------------

3 things I did today:

01. _____

02. _____

03. _____

Favorite thing I ate today:

_____

One person I met today (name, age, where they are from):

_____

One thing I learned about the world today:

_____

One thing I learned about myself today:

_____

One thing I will do different tomorrow:

_____

General thoughts about today:

_____

_____

_____

DATE: _____   **PLACE:** _____   **BUDGET:** _____

"Absorb what is useful, discard what is not, add what is uniquely your own."

— Bruce Lee

3 things I did today:

01. _____

02. _____

03. _____

Favorite thing I ate today:

_____

One person I met today (name, age, where they are from):

_____

One thing I learned about the world today:

_____

One thing I learned about myself today:

_____

One thing I will do different tomorrow:

_____

General thoughts about today:

_____

_____

_____

DATE: _____   **PLACE:** _____   **BUDGET:** _____

---

3 things I did today:

01. _____

02. _____

03. _____

Favorite thing I ate today:

_____

One person I met today (name, age, where they are from):

_____

One thing I learned about the world today:

_____

One thing I learned about myself today:

_____

One thing I will do different tomorrow:

_____

General thoughts about today:

_____

_____

_____

DATE: _____   **PLACE:** _____   **BUDGET:** _____

"Tell me and I forget. Teach me and I remember. Involve me and I learn."
— Benjamin Franklin

3 things I did today:

01. _____

02. _____

03. _____

Favorite thing I ate today:

_____

One person I met today (name, age, where they are from):

_____

One thing I learned about the world today:

_____

One thing I learned about myself today:

_____

One thing I will do different tomorrow:

_____

General thoughts about today:

_____

_____

_____

DATE: _____ **PLACE:** _____ **BUDGET:** _____

———————————— ✦ ————————————

3 things I did today:

01. _____

02. _____

03. _____

Favorite thing I ate today:

_____

One person I met today (name, age, where they are from):

_____

One thing I learned about the world today:

_____

One thing I learned about myself today:

_____

One thing I will do different tomorrow:

_____

General thoughts about today:

_____

_____

_____

DATE: _____ PLACE: _____ BUDGET: _____

"Half the fun of the travel is the esthetic of lostness."
— Ray Bradbury

3 things I did today:

01. _____

02. _____

03. _____

Favorite thing I ate today:

_____

One person I met today (name, age, where they are from):

_____

One thing I learned about the world today:

_____

One thing I learned about myself today:

_____

One thing I will do different tomorrow:

_____

General thoughts about today:

_____

_____

_____

DATE: _____   **PLACE:** _____   **BUDGET:** _____

---

3 things I did today:

01. _____

02. _____

03. _____

Favorite thing I ate today:

_____

One person I met today (name, age, where they are from):

_____

One thing I learned about the world today:

_____

One thing I learned about myself today:

_____

One thing I will do different tomorrow:

_____

General thoughts about today:

_____

_____

_____

"If we were meant to stay in one place, we'd have roots instead of feet."
— Rachel Wolchin

3 things I did today:

01. _____

02. _____

03. _____

Favorite thing I ate today:

_____

One person I met today (name, age, where they are from):

_____

One thing I learned about the world today:

_____

One thing I learned about myself today:

_____

One thing I will do different tomorrow:

_____

General thoughts about today:

_____

_____

_____

DATE: _____   **PLACE:** _____   **BUDGET:** _____

————————————◆————————————

3 things I did today:

01. _____

02. _____

03. _____

Favorite thing I ate today:

_____

One person I met today (name, age, where they are from):

_____

One thing I learned about the world today:

_____

One thing I learned about myself today:

_____

One thing I will do different tomorrow:

_____

General thoughts about today:

_____

_____

_____

DATE: _____   PLACE: _____   BUDGET: _____

"You don't have to be rich to travel well."
— Eugene Fodor

3 things I did today:

01. _____

02. _____

03. _____

Favorite thing I ate today:

_____

One person I met today (name, age, where they are from):

_____

One thing I learned about the world today:

_____

One thing I learned about myself today:

_____

One thing I will do different tomorrow:

_____

General thoughts about today:

_____

_____

_____

DATE: _____ **PLACE:** _____ **BUDGET:** _____

---◆---

3 things I did today:

01. _____

02. _____

03. _____

Favorite thing I ate today:

_____

One person I met today (name, age, where they are from):

_____

One thing I learned about the world today:

_____

One thing I learned about myself today:

_____

One thing I will do different tomorrow:

_____

General thoughts about today:

_____

_____

_____

DATE: _____   **PLACE:** _____   **BUDGET:** _____

"Travel and change of place impart new vigor to the mind."

— Seneca

3 things I did today:

01. _____

02. _____

03. _____

Favorite thing I ate today:

_____

One person I met today (name, age, where they are from):

_____

One thing I learned about the world today:

_____

One thing I learned about myself today:

_____

One thing I will do different tomorrow:

_____

General thoughts about today:

_____

_____

_____

3 things I did today:

01. _____

02. _____

03. _____

Favorite thing I ate today:

_____

One person I met today (name, age, where they are from):

_____

One thing I learned about the world today:

_____

One thing I learned about myself today:

_____

One thing I will do different tomorrow:

_____

General thoughts about today:

_____

_____

_____

POST-TRIP THOUGHTS

—

Now that you are back from your trip, think about all you
accomplished. You may be thinking about all the things you
missed but the world is a big place and you can never see it all
(and it's a good excuse to use for another trip). Use the prompts
below to remember all you accomplished. Be proud of it.

"Travel isn't always pretty. It isn't always comfortable. Sometimes it hurts, it even breaks your heart. But that's okay. The journey changes you; it should change you. It leaves marks on your memory, on your consciousness, on your heart, and on your body. You take something with you. Hopefully, you leave something good behind."

— Anthony Bourdain

On this trip, I went to:

_____

_____

_____

_____

My favorite place was:

_____

_____

My least favorite place was:

_____

_____

My favorite experience was (and why):

_____

_____

_____

My least favorite experience was (and why):

_____

_____

_____

On this trip, I learned about the world:

_____

_____

_____

On this trip, I learned about myself:

_____

_____

_____

On my next trip, I will:

_____

_____

_____

On this trip I spent:

_____

_____

_____

ABOUT US

—

About My Travel Journal

After years of traveling around the world and documenting trips through lengthy blog posts and social media photos, Matt Kepnes (AKA Nomadic Matt), still felt there was something missing about the way we document our travels. Though our digital methods of documentation are great, there's something truly special about putting pen to paper that allows us to forge deeper memories.

My Travel Journal was created to help guide you through the transformative thoughts, emotions, and experiences you have while on the road. Through simple prompts, you'll be able to document and remember your travels in new ways.

About Matt Kepnes

Matt Kepnes is an American travel blogger, author, and New York Times best-selling writer. He was born in Boston. In 2005, after meeting backpackers in Thailand, he came home, quit his job, finished his MBA, and began traveling the world and writing about his experiences on his blog, Nomadic Matt. Today, Matt has helped millions of people travel better, cheaper, and longer through his website. He's also authored two books, *How to Travel the World on $50 a Day* and *Ten Years a Nomad*. When he's not traveling the world, he lives in Austin, TX.

Follow Us On Social Media

TikTok: @rememberyourtravels
Instagram: @rememberyourtravels
Twitter: @rememberyourtravels